Chicken Soup for the Soul.

Devotional Stories for Mothers and Grandmothers

Chicken Soup for the Soul: Devotional Stories for Mothers and Grandmothers
101 Devotions with Scripture, Real-Life Stories & Custom Prayers
Susan M. Heim and Karen C. Talcott. Foreword by Lisa Whelchel

Published by Chicken Soup for the Soul, LLC www.chickensoup.com

Previously published in 2010 as *Chicken Soup for the Soul: Devotional Stories for Mothers*

The publisher gratefully acknowledges the many publishers and individuals who granted Chicken Soup for the Soul permission to reprint the cited material.

Front cover photo courtesy of iStockphoto.com/ Daniel_Keuck (© Daniel_Keuck)
Interior illustrations coutesy of iStockphoto.com/ Bokasana (© Bokasana)

Cover and Interior Daniel Zaccari

Distributed to the booktrade by Simon & Schuster. SAN: 200-2442

Publisher's Cataloging-in-Publication Data

Names: Heim, Susan M., editor. | Talcott, Susan M., editor. | Whelchel, Lisa, foreword
        author.
Title: Chicken soup for the soul : devotional stories for mothers and grandmothers,
        101 devotions with scripture, real-life stories & custom prayers /
        Susan M. Heim & Karen Talcott; foreword by Lisa Whelchel.
Description: Cos Cob, CT: Chicken Soup for the Soul, LLC.
Identifiers: LCCN: 2022942112 | ISBN: 978-1-61159-096-8 (hardcover)
Subjects: LCSH Mothers--Religious life--Literary collections. | Christian life--
        Anecdotes. | Mothers--Prayers and devotions. | BISAC RELIGION / Christian
        Living / Devotional | RELIGION / Christian Living / Women's Interests
Classification: LCC BV4847 .C45 2022 | DDC 242.6/431--dc23

PRINTED IN THE UNITED STATES OF AMERICA
on acid∞free paper

27 26 25 24 23 22   01 02 03 04 05 06 07 08 09 10

Devotional Stories for Mothers
and
Grandmothers

101 Devotions with Scripture,
Real-life Stories & Custom Prayers

Susan M. Heim & Karen Talcott
Foreword by Lisa Whelchel

CSS

Chicken Soup for the Soul, LLC
Cos Cob, CT

Changing lives one story at a time ®
www.chickensoup.com

Table of Contents

❶
~Treasured Moments~

❷
~God's Guiding Hand~

❸

~Loving Through Tears~

❹

~In the Beginning~

❺

~Lessons from Our Kids~

❻

~Comfort Through Prayer~

❼

~Help from Above~

8
~Surrendering Our Worries~

9
~Whispers of Wisdom~

10
~Giving Them Wings~

⑪

~Celebrating Our Families~

Foreword

For most of my growing-up years, I played the character "Blair" on a sitcom named *The Facts of Life*. We filmed the last episode of the show in March of 1988. I was married in July of '88. I got pregnant in '89. Then I had a child in '90, '91 and '92.

That means I had three babies in diapers, ran after three preschoolers, homeschooled three children, survived three teenagers, and am recently the mother of three baby birds who have left the nest. Life is suddenly very different for me.

I remember when my children were babies and some well-meaning older woman (probably the age I am now!) would counsel me with, "Enjoy every minute; they grow up so fast." I must be honest… I was tempted to slap her with a Wet Wipe! That was so not my experience. From my perspective, the days seemed to drag on forever until the magical moment when the last bath was taken, the final cup of water was fetched, and I could at long last do what I wanted to do. Well, in theory I could. The truth was, I was too tired to do anything but fall into bed and feel guilty about the dirty dishes still in the sink and the pile of laundry I really meant to fold that day.

Guilt was a primary emotion throughout those years. There just didn't seem to be enough of me to go around. I was either falling asleep with crunchy kitchen floors or I was berating myself for popping in a video or two (or two hundred). I always had the best intentions of getting out of my pajamas and into something sexy before my husband came home, but, inevitably, he counted himself lucky if I met him at the door in my sweats and T-shirt, ponytail Scrunchie, and a little mascara.

Finding time to do anything for myself during the day felt like a thing of the past and an even more distant future. So I concentrated on trying harder to be a better mother, wife, and friend. There was just one tiny problem. There were many days when I had nothing left to give by 9:00 in the morning! And, for the rest of the day, I was running on empty.

I believe that is a common experience for mothers. We are, by nature, caregivers. This is wonderful, and I wouldn't trade my role as mother for any Academy Award leading role. But, as mothers, we must learn how to receive. We tend to give and give and give, but if we don't take time to receive, we can burn out. Then we end up giving out of the dregs. We scrape the bottom of the barrel to give a little more, but our offering is often tainted by irritation and exhaustion and a strain of emptiness.

I am so proud of you for picking up this book, *Chicken Soup for the Soul: Devotional Stories for Mothers and Grandmothers*. Even taking the time to read a book means you are doing something for yourself. The irony is that when we take time to care for ourselves, we are better able to care for our families—out of the overflow rather than the overwhelmed.

I want to encourage you to give yourself permission if you need it (and, sadly, so many of us do) to take a few minutes every day to pick up this book and fill up your soul. It is the perfect book for busy mothers. Each story is just long enough to read while you are waiting in the carpool line, or in the bleachers at soccer practice, or in the sanctuary behind the blessedly closed bathroom door.

In the throes of child-rearing, I often felt guilty for not having time to read anything other than parenting books (which usually made me feel even more guilty, by the way). I felt like I should be reading my Bible more, the newspaper occasionally, or maybe even the seemingly decadent choice of an Oprah's Book Club selection.

On the other side of young motherhood, may I offer a word of advice? Be gentle with yourself during these chaotic days. This season really is shorter than you think at the moment. There will come a day when you can read a whole book that doesn't rhyme. In the meantime, thank God for books like those in the Chicken Soup for the Soul series.

Allow me to illustrate, once again, from my personal experience. My oldest child, Tucker, is away in college. During finals week, I sent him twenty-five Cup-a-Soups. Would he have preferred Mom's homemade chicken noodle soup? Absolutely. Was that an option? No. Was he thrilled to receive the box of instant soups? Completely.

I am thrilled to present this book to you. It is perfectly sized, tailor-made, especially designed, specifically written just for you at this busy season of your life. Someday, you can read *War and Peace* and make homemade chicken noodle soup. Until then, *Chicken Soup for the Soul: Devotional Stories for Mothers and Grandmothers* is just what the doctor—and this older mother—ordered. Enjoy.

— Lisa Whelchel —
Actor, Speaker, and Author of
Creative Correction and *Friendship for Grown-Ups*

Introduction

There is a time for everything, and a
season for every activity under heaven.
~Ecclesiastes 3:1

Every year, we eagerly await each new season and its unique gifts. In the same way, throughout our lives, we celebrate the distinct seasons of motherhood and the blessings of each step along the way. We start our parenting journey in the spring when life is about expectancy. The seeds we planted have resulted in life, and new blooms emerge all around us. This is the time when we are pregnant and raising young children. Life is full of highs and lows—April showers and May flowers—and our lives seem eternally busy. We long for sleep, wish for sanity, and through it all tend to these little seedlings that are our children.

Summer comes along, and with it the hot days and cooler nights. Our children are growing and testing our patience with their own attitudes and rebellious ideas. Some days, in the heat of the moment, arguments erupt over their desire for independence and their struggles to forge their own identity. And yet, in the quiet evening, our teenagers come to us seeking peace and forgiveness. They still need us to water their roots and offer the unconditional love that only a mother can give.

In the fall, the leaves change color, and the world seems to slow down. Our children are grown now and moving away, starting careers and even their own families. Some days, the wind blows cool as we realize our important job of mothering is almost over. They have left home, and our lives begin to feel barren. It is the time when we look to fill our lives with other passions and desires that have been pushed off to the side while we raised our children. Our crops are now sown, but our field can be used again for new pursuits and interests.

And, finally, winter comes. We move slower now, and the days are much quieter. We are the grandmothers, and our children are now the mothers and fathers. They move at the fast pace of spring and summer, but we watch it all with a sense of peace and acceptance. Our hearts are content knowing that our own seeds have sprouted and grown, and are now producing new little seeds in God's earthly kingdom.

Wise King Solomon wrote a thoughtful and beautiful scripture more than 2,000 years ago illustrating the changes that occur in our lives. Read it today with fresh eyes from a mother's perspective. Although we cannot escape the passing of the seasons, we know that God watches out for us and guides us through every season of motherhood.

> There is a time for everything,
> and a season for every activity under heaven:
> a time to be born and a time to die,
> a time to plant and a time to uproot,
> a time to kill and a time to heal,
> a time to tear down and a time to build,
> a time to weep and a time to laugh,
> a time to mourn and a time to dance,
> a time to scatter stones and a time to gather them,
> a time to embrace and a time to refrain,
> a time to search and a time to give up,
> a time to keep and a time to throw away,
> a time to tear and a time to mend,
> a time to be silent and a time to speak,
> a time to love and a time to hate,
> a time for war and a time for peace.
> ~*Ecclesiastes 3:1-8*

This book is filled with stories celebrating the seasons of motherhood, from pregnancy and the early years to the trials of adolescence and the resulting empty nest. Whatever season you may be in, you'll find that each story and accompanying Bible verse has a lesson to teach. And the common thread through it all is the knowledge that God is present in every season, whether it turns out to be stormy or filled with sunshine.

There are several ways in which you can read *Chicken Soup for the Soul: Devotional Stories for Mothers and Grandmothers*:

- **Start at the beginning!** Spend a little time with God each day by starting at the beginning of the book and reading a story each day for inspiration.

- **Pray for guidance.** Holding the book closed, pray for God to guide you to just the right devotional that you need to read that day. Randomly open the book and see where the Spirit leads!

- **Select a topic.** If you're dealing with a particular problem, scroll through the table of contents and turn to the appropriate chapter. Select a devotional that applies to your situation.

We feel confident that the words of wisdom from the women in this book will warm your heart and show you that God is your partner through every season of motherhood.

— Susan and Karen —

1

A Handful of Hope

*[Love] always protects, always trusts,
always hopes, always perseveres.*
~1 Corinthians 13:7

"Goodbye, Trevor," I said to my nine-year-old son as he trudged through the snowy yard on his way to school. But, as usual, he didn't turn around or acknowledge my words. He had just been diagnosed with Pervasive Developmental Disorder (PDD), which explained his lack of expression and communication. But it left us with more questions, more pain, and more worry for the future. Since the age of three, he had almost completely stopped talking. He wouldn't even look at me and smile.

Everything had to be the same every day, including his black mittens. No other pair would do. But this morning I couldn't find his black mittens, so he had to wear a spare pair. He had become angry with me and slammed the door.

I watched his little blond head bob up and down behind the fence as he continued walking to school, gesturing with his hands. He talks to himself all the time. If only he would share a story or two with me,

I thought, as I left the window and returned to finish the breakfast dishes.

Tears dropped onto the table as I wiped the spot where Trevor sat each morning for breakfast. He routinely blurted out inappropriate messages to his cereal, but I was merely the invisible robot that served him.

"Goodnight, I love you," was only a rote saying that he recited each night at bedtime after he brushed his teeth and put on his pajamas.

A knock at the door interrupted my sullen thoughts. I wiped the tears from my face and wondered who could be here so early.

When I opened the door, Trevor stood trembling on the doorstep.

"Trevor! What's wrong? Did you forget your books?"

He didn't answer. He stepped in and looked up at me. His cheeks were a rosy pink from the cool February day.

"Mommy," he began.

I held my breath. For several years, he hadn't looked me straight in the eye or called me by name.

"Yes?" I whispered. I slowly lowered to my knees to be at his eye level. If I moved too quickly, I would shatter this fragile moment.

His bright blue eyes grew shiny, and a tear slipped down his round cheeks.

"Mommy, I'm sorry," he said.

He only spoke three simple words, but his soul had opened. He had talked to me from his heart. He showed emotion.

Then his face hardened, and he turned and ran. The moment was over. Iron bars separated my heart and his once again.

I stayed in that spot on the floor and pressed a handful of hope to my heart. It was like a door had opened for the first time, and he had pulled me through it into his world.

It didn't happen again for a long time, but I always knew it would. I knew that Trevor was in there. I knew he would come out again. That moment sustained me for years. Sometimes, he smiles so brightly that the chains of autism rattle their retreat for a few moments, and we connect.

All it took was three words, a tear, and his round blue eyes looking into mine. And I will always be grateful to God for giving me this little spark of hope.

— Pam Mytroen —

My Prayer

Thank you, Lord, for the gift of hope.
May you give hope to others who
are raising developmentally challenged children.
Help us to see the perfect soul
that resides within each of our children.
Amen.

That Praying Family

Therefore, whoever humbles himself
like this child is the greatest
in the kingdom of heaven.
~Matthew 18:4

It was the tail end of our little family getaway, just my children and me. We were tired, cranky, and aching for home and our own beds. We stopped in Reno at a circus-themed hotel for our last "hotel night."

Our first stop was the restaurant. When the food arrived, I reached for my napkin and watched all but one of my kids reach for their forks. Glancing over at my five-year-old, I was surprised to see him sitting quietly. (He does NOTHING quietly.)

"We need to pray," he said.

My little one's clear blue eyes told me he was very serious about this. My other children immediately grasped the situation and began to giggle at the thought of praying right here in Reno, Nevada, in the middle of a circus/casino/restaurant.

"My turn," Noah told us. Then he solemnly closed his eyes and began his prayer.

I felt a giggle coming on, too, and had to suppress it. I knew we were most likely the only people who had ever prayed in this place. But I also struggled to control my mirth because Noah is deaf, his prayer was entirely in sign language, and he is very expressive! My giggles were quickly replaced with tenderness as my heart swelled with pride. Noah blessed the food and gave thanks for it, but he also blessed his mommy, his kitty, the hotel, his fork, trains in general, his grandparents, our car's tires, and pretty much anything and anyone he had ever met.

I felt the people seated around us grow silent as Noah prayed. And as I watched his little hands talking to God, tears filled my eyes. How blessed I am to be the mother of this incredible little spirit! The silence around us was magnificent as everyone in the restaurant watched a child offer a prayer. I wondered how many of them had ever witnessed a prayer in sign language, let alone in this unlikely place. I felt the Lord's presence with us, and a warmth and sense of immense joy settled around me. As the prayer continued, I realized what an example we, as a family, were setting. And I felt ashamed that I hadn't thought of praying as we normally do at each meal.

As the "amens" rounded our table, I stole a peek at the tables around us. An elderly man with Elvis sideburns mouthed "amen" to me, and his smile told me that Noah's prayer had touched more than my own heart. Everyone at the restaurant seemed to sense the same peace, and the meals were eaten with quiet reverence. As the man with sideburns passed our table on the way out, he gave Noah a thumbs-up—the universal sign for "good job." Noah grinned at the man, spaghetti sauce on his cheeks, even though he had no idea of the impact he'd had on the man. I know it will be a while before that man forgets Noah or his prayer.

After dinner, it fully hit me what a difference my little guy's prayer had made in this corner of the world. A circus act was beginning, and the kids and I crowded in to see. As I held Noah up for a better view, a lady crowded in next to us. Glancing at me, she put her arm across my shoulders and said, "Oh! You're that praying family!"

I looked at my golden boy, smiled, and couldn't think of anything better to be. That praying family.

— Susan Farr-Fahncke —

My Prayer

Dear Father, let me show in my everyday life
that there is no wrong time or place to pray;
you are always listening.
Help me to remember that I am an example
to those around me.
And through my actions,
they may come closer to you.
Amen.

3

A Window of Light

When Jesus spoke again to the people,
he said, "I am the light of the world.
Whoever follows me will never walk in
darkness, but will have the light of life."
~John 8:12

I have three children. Two live with me here on Earth, and one lives with God in Heaven. But wherever they are, they are my children — all three — and I love them.

When I was thirty-seven years old, I had my third and last child — a baby daughter. She tiptoed into my life on a warm August evening and then left as quickly as she had come, seeing the light of only one morning. She was nine hours and one minute old. But in my heart she had lived a lifetime and a day. In the days that followed, it was hard for me to see anything through my tears. I was heartbroken. Devastated. I didn't know if I would make it.

But one Sunday morning, a few months later, something strange and wonderful happened. I was sitting in my family room, looking out at boxes of red geraniums I had just planted, when an exceptionally bright beam of light flashed across the sliding glass door. The light quickly bolted toward the back of the kitchen, leaving me breathless.

Without hesitation, I got up from the couch and followed it. The light had settled in the center of the kitchen window, appearing in the form of a beautiful dove, its perfectly sculpted wings painted with sunlight. Awestruck, I called for my seven-year-old daughter and four-year-old son. I wanted to share this moment with them.

"Hurry!" I called out. "Come see the beautiful white bird!"

They scampered down the hallway and into the kitchen where the brilliant rays from the dove warmed the room. My little son grabbed my hand, his eyes fixed on the window. The unexpected Sunday visitor softly fluttered its wings, as if it wanted to come in.

"Let's let it in, Mamma!" my daughter cried.

"How will we get it back outside again?" I said, not knowing what to do. "Maybe it wants to be free."

Where did this bird come from? Why was it at my window? Had it seen my tears? Did it have a message for me?

We stood there bathed in this circle of light, totally caught up in the dove's presence. Ribbons of peace, joy and contentment enveloped me. I gently embraced my children, grateful for their presence in my life. And for a moment, I felt like everything was right with the world… like all three of my children were standing there with me. All three. My heart was full.

And then the light seemed to disappear as quickly and miraculously as it had appeared. I didn't see the dove fly away. It was there… and then it wasn't. It simply slipped away, blending quietly into the morning sun.

The following day, I dropped my daughter off at her second-grade classroom. I told my daughter's teacher, Sister Roberta, what we had seen. She listened to my story as if every word were a prayer, serenity gathering in the neatly pressed folds of her veil. She was convinced that this magnificent white bird was the soul of my baby daughter coming back to Earth to thank me for giving her eternal life. What a beautiful sentiment, I thought. And what's more… I believed her.

— Lola Di Giulio De Maci —

My Prayer

Watch over my children,
Lord, wherever they may be.
Sometimes, I find it difficult
to let go of their hands,
wanting to keep them close to me.
Encircle them in your light
so that where they are,
you will also be.
Amen.

4

A Butterfly Moment with Mike

*You open your hand and satisfy
the desires of every living thing.*
~Psalm 145:16

"Mom, come here!" Michael called. I was stirring spaghetti sauce, but hearing the urgency in his voice, I hurried to his bedroom. "What do you want?" I asked, glimpsing the unmade bed littered with clothing.

"Quick!" he said.

He was holding a cocoon that dangled from a string while balancing a jar in his other hand.

"I'm going to tie this up. If it falls, will you catch it?"

Obediently, I cupped my hand beneath the fragile object. I studied my teenage son's face, noting the concern in his piercing blue eyes and the earnestness with which he worked nimble fingers to tie the string to a branch overhead.

"There, I hope it's all right. The butterfly is already beginning to peep through its protective wall," he sighed.

Where had I been? How did this happen? A cocoon inside our home. This was the least of the problems, I decided, scanning the room. The branch, sprayed with gold paint, hung from the ceiling. Posters, books, and papers lay scattered about, like debris after an explosion. In the corner, I noticed a book on organic gardening, a half-painted seagull, a bottle of straw flowers, and rocks glued with seashells.

Had my job taken me so far from home that I had missed seeing what was happening here? My first inclination was to complain about the clutter and chaos, but Michael was studying his newest jewel so intently that he hadn't seen my displeasure.

"Do you see the wings?" he asked. A tiny monarch butterfly was about to be born.

I breathed deeply and tried to block out the messy room. My son's focus was on the new birth. His life was alive — overflowing with the natural world. My mind drifted back to memories of him as a small boy, always so interested in his surroundings.

"Look, Mom," Michael squealed. The butterfly fluttered on Michael's open palm.

"This is amazing," I marveled.

I had nearly missed seeing my teenage son's inner spirit. That day, I saw a compassionate young man.

This must be the way God sees us, I mused. In the midst of our busy lives, often filled with clutter and confusion, how often do we miss the beauty of God's work and the palm of His hand beneath us?

— Phyllis Cochran —

My Prayer

*Lord, help us to blot out the clutter around us
and see the inner beauty in our children.
May their desire to embrace the beauty of nature
and all of God's creation never fade away.
Amen.*

Crazy Normal

*From the fullness of his grace we have
all received one blessing after another.*
~*John 1:16*

Crazy is our new normal. With two teenage boys and three little boys, our family is in perpetual motion—to the baseball diamond, track field, piano lessons, and Bible club. Even though we've limited each boy's activities and try our best to defend our family time, it seems that we're in a constant state of flight.

"Embrace it. Roll with it," my husband, Lonny, says. "It's going to be like this for a while."

He's right. It's likely that life will continue to careen full-throttle forward before it slows down. But I remembered the still, quiet days that our family used to enjoy. I missed long walks through the park when we clutched the boys' little hands and took time to feel the sun on our shoulders. I longed for lazy Saturday afternoons under the oak in our backyard, when towheaded boys built forts of sticks and castles of sand. I wanted to slip back a few years, when busyness was the exception and not the rule.

One night, after a particularly full day and evening Little League games, our family gathered on the porch for ice cream. Two parents, two teens, and three small boys piled on one old swing and a couple of rocking chairs.

We were together, in one place, for a small slice of time.

The moon was full. The Mississippi River, flowing past our home, was smooth as glass. The creak of the swing was the only sound. Lonny's arm draped across my shoulders in the comfortable way it had for twenty years. I wrapped my own arms around the son who sat on my lap and breathed deeply to inhale his little-boy scent—dirt and sweat and a hint of Tide.

My heart was still and content.

I realized that while crazy is our new normal, God is faithful to provide blessings along the way. They may look different from before, but they are still there—even if they're in the form of a single moment on the porch, when Rocky Road runs in sweet rivers down small, brown arms, and the night drapes our porch and frames our family.

Maybe I just needed the eyes to see.

— Shawnelle Eliasen —

My Prayer

Lord, you are faithful to provide everything that my family needs. In a crazy, busy time of life, help me to appreciate the quiet times and see your blessings.
Amen.

The Greatest Gift

"But blessed is the man who trusts in the LORD,
whose confidence is in him. He will be like a tree
planted by the water that sends out
its roots by the stream...."
~Jeremiah 17:7-8

My mother's health took a turn for the worse two weeks before my cross-country trip to visit my daughter, Nicole. When I had booked my flight six months earlier, my mother's condition was stable, and she had encouraged me to go. But now as I sat by her bedside, I questioned if going to California was in my mother's best interest.

"Don't cancel your trip to see Nicole," she said.

"I'm afraid to leave you," was my honest response.

"I have nurses round the clock. I'm in good hands," she assured me. "Nothing is going to happen to me. Go see Nicole."

I tried to smile, but only nodded.

"Do you still have my wedding ring?" she asked.

"Of course." My mother had given me her jewelry to take care of when she was admitted into a nursing facility.

"I want you to bring my wedding ring to Nicole," she said.

I was deeply touched and wiped away tears. My heart's desire had always been for my only daughter, my mother's only granddaughter, to have her ring.

"Nicole has always loved my ring, and I want her to have it," she said.

"Momma, it will mean so much to her that you are giving it to her. It would be an honor to bring it with me."

I knew then that I had to travel to California. The night before I left, my mother's condition was the same.

"Did you clean my ring?" she asked.

"Yes, Momma. It's sparkling."

I told her that I was going to wear her ring until Nicole noticed it, and then I would tell her that Maw-Maw had sent it to her.

For most of the flight, I gazed at the ring, anticipating what this gift would mean to Nicole. Excitement welled up in me as I imagined Nicole's reaction, but fear haunted me as I thought about my mother's failing health.

It wasn't until we returned from the airport to Nicole's apartment that she noticed the ring. I was petting her dog when she gasped, grabbing my hand.

"Maw-Maw's ring!"

"Yes, my love," I said. "She wants you to have it."

In an eruption of tears, Nicole hugged me. I slipped the ring from my finger. She shook her head in disbelief. I wasn't sure she was going to take it from me.

"Maw-Maw is going to live for a long time," she sobbed. "She doesn't need to give me this now."

"She wants you to have it. It is wonderful that she can give it to you while she is still with us."

Nicole let me place the ring on her finger. She held out her hand to admire it and then ran to telephone my mother.

On the last morning of my trip, my greatest fear was realized. My mother's condition had worsened. It would be twenty-four hours before I could be at her bedside.

For the next eleven days, I watched my mother abandon herself to the inevitable, while keeping Nicole informed. I was privileged to be with my mother to the very end with a blessed assurance of where she was going.

Nicole proudly wore my mother's ring to the funeral and spoke at the service. She gave a beautiful tribute to her grandmother's life. I was privileged to watch my child demonstrate sincere love and respect. As the ring sparkled on Nicole's finger, I knew that my mother's gift was much more than precious jewelry. It was a testimony of love between mothers and daughters.

— Debbie Cannizzaro —

My Prayer

Father, help us to see that the greatest gift
we can give our children is love.
We thank you that, in sowing the seeds,
we reap an abundant harvest of love in return.
Amen.

1

A Wrinkled Kiss

God is not unjust; he will not forget your work and
the love you have shown him as you have
helped his people and continue to help them.
~Hebrews 6:10

I was not nervous, but neither did I know what to expect. I was taking my children to a nursing home to serve the residents. It was an opportunity presented through a group of people in my church who regularly reached out in love to the elderly. Though my children, ages seven and five, had not been around older people very often, I was pretty sure they would be comfortable enough to interact positively without being too frightened.

We were asked to help the residents paint a pot for their garden, and then serve cookies and coffee. My kids are always up for a craft project, and anything having to do with paint especially excites them. They gladly plopped down at one of the tables next to the residents and began to paint little animals onto the clay pots, with minimal apprehensive glances at the shaking hands painting beside them.

It was during "snack time"—as my son, Josiah, endearingly referred to it—that I was stunned and filled with pride all at once. After passing out cookies, my children finished their crunchy sweets in no time, and began to follow me as I meandered and mingled among the residents. If you've ever been to a nursing home, you'll be able to relate to the fragrant wet-diaper-mixed-with-antiseptic-soap-and-Bengay smell that permeated our noses, even as we tasted the cookies. For me, a former certified nursing assistant, it was no big deal, but I feared that my kids and their hypersensitive young noses were not going to tolerate the environment much longer. It was then, while I was predicting how many more minutes they would last before whining to go home, that I observed one of the most beautiful things I've ever seen. No matter how long I live, I'll never forget it.

One particularly fetid woman had taken a fancy to my son, even being so bold as to hold his hand and squeeze his cheeks. (My son is extremely handsome, bearing the cutest freckles splayed across his sweet little face.) She would beckon him over to her if he wandered too far away. The lines were etched so deeply in her face that I guessed she must have been at least ninety-five years old. Her hands held the beauty of age spots and long, twisted fingers that shook when she reached up to touch him. I was just about to retrieve our jackets and tell them it was time for us to leave when this lovely, endearing woman pointed to her face and puckered her lips to ask him for a kiss.

I felt my eyes widening in curiosity at what he would do. While I could not condone any disgust or rudeness from my son, neither could I force him to do anything awkward or embarrassing. And while I stood there pondering my next move, Josiah amazingly and without hesitation reached out, braced his hand on her wheelchair, and puckered his own pink lips to meet hers. Gentle. Sweet. Unafraid. A smile filled her ancient face, and her delight shone just as bright as if she were decades younger. My charming son could not help but smile in response. Needless to say, my proud tears slid down to the upturned corners of my mouth.

We left that day different from when we had arrived. God had revealed His tender love through my son's courage and grace. It is a wrinkled kiss I'll never forget.

— Robyn Langdon —

My Prayer

Today and every day, Father,
let me show others what unconditional love
and compassion look like.
Through my acts,
may they know I belong to the family of God.
Amen.

Bouquet of Weeds

"But the one who received the seed that fell on good soil is the man who hears the word and understands it. He produces a crop, yielding a hundred, sixty or thirty times what was sown."
~Matthew 13:23

My son, Doug, loves weeds. He loves weeds as much as clouds love the sky! He taps them. He folds and molds them. I've even found them under his pillow. The one nice thing about it is that he isn't particular; he likes any color, size, shape or form.

"Doug, what are you doing with that weed in the house?" I questioned impatiently one spring day. "I'm cleaning, and I've already thrown away a big handful of weeds that I've found all over. Now take that old thing outside and don't bring another one in the house. Do you understand?"

"All right!" exclaimed Doug, with a look of persistence in his eyes. "But they aren't just old things. Anyway, why did God make 'em?"

As Doug turned his back and marched out into the yard with his treasure, I pondered the question on his six-year-old mind, knowing he wanted and expected an answer from me. Why does God make weeds?

"So," Doug said, reentering the house and placing his hands firmly on his hips, "why did God make 'em?"

I knelt beside Doug and took his hands. "I think God made weeds for little boys to enjoy. I think He knew that you would be one of the special ones who would love and find beauty in weeds."

A big smile spread across Doug's face. I could tell that he burned with that inner glow of feeling special, something we all need to experience, whether we are two or seventy-two.

"You see, Doug, not everyone thinks weeds are beautiful. It takes a special eye to see their beauty."

"Do your eyes like 'em, Mom?"

"Well, my eyes do, but I like them best outside because I don't like to pick them up all over the house. Maybe you can pick them, plant them, and play with them outside. I think I'd like them even more."

"Okay," was Doug's unconcerned reply as he turned and flew back out of the house.

Did our little conversation work miracles? Are you kidding? I still find weeds in the house, but I don't get upset about it anymore. I realize that, somewhere in our childhood, most of us are fashioned into what others think we should be and should like. As adults, we no longer find time to view the world through the eyes of a child, or see the beauty and purpose of weeds. My son sees weeds just as they are. He does not question their beauty but rather their entitlement to be a part of God's plan.

I have just received a lovely gift from my son: a bouquet of weeds. I shall put them in a crystal vase and place them on our dinner table where we will say grace, thanking God for family, food… and weeds.

— Kathie Harrington —

My Prayer

*Dear God, what a blessing it is that our children
can see the beauty in an ordinary weed.
I admire how they look beyond the flowers
and find the good in even the simplest of plants.
Help me to learn from this childlike wonder
and see the world as you do —
a perfect creation.
Amen.*

9

I Salute You, Mother

"Many women do noble things,
but you surpass them all."
~Proverbs 31:29

When my four boys were under the age of seven, and I was too tired to think straight, I abandoned reason altogether. I went to a café for breakfast. With the kids. Without my husband. I didn't ordinarily take them to restaurants because I don't like paying for a bad time. But a friend with only two kids, aged six and seven, suggested it, and I didn't want to decline. Honestly, she probably said the magic words "my treat," and I couldn't resist. So I drew in a deep breath and prepared myself for syrup in the hair and water streaming across the table, while trying to remain relaxed enough to nurse a baby.

Other than the standard soggy islands of napkins on the table and enough food for the next day's breakfast on the floor, our dining experience went remarkably well. I even managed a few bites. As we were leaving, I collected the endless baby accoutrements, heaving the diaper bag with such force it almost propelled me in a circle. Then I collected the small humans, carrying the smallest of the lot, and ushered the noisy line toward the door.

As I passed the table of an elderly man, he smiled and told me my boys reminded him of his family. "I have four boys," he said. He was dining alone, and I felt obliged to stop. He straightened his silverware and then looked up at me. His slow movement in my frenzied world heightened my impatience. I was tired, hungry, and losing kids out the front door. I hoped my friend would corral them. I bounced the baby on my hip, anticipating that one of us would need calming soon.

"Make sure they grow up to respect themselves," he said. I stopped bouncing the baby. That was not a line I was expecting. "They will learn that from you," he added.

My teaching hadn't really gotten beyond "don't bite" and "get it in the potty." But he was right. My boys would learn many things from me that I wasn't deliberately teaching, at least not now. I told the man I understood the importance of my role as teacher.

"They're also learning about love from you," he said.

I hadn't really thought about that. Tender moments I'd shared with my boys sprang to mind, endless gazing sessions where we'd get lost in each others' eyes, soft words of love carried on warm breath. Yes, true. Mothers have a unique intimacy and corporal attentiveness to their children, an extension, perhaps, of the physical bond in pregnancy.

Although the man was quiet, his introspective manner told me he wasn't done. I shifted the baby on my hip, as he remained lost in thought. Chaos was due to track me down any minute. I raised my eyebrows. And…?

Then he looked at me with humility and what seemed to be adoration, not the look I typically elicit from strangers in a restaurant. His reverent gaze lingered, instantly exposing me as the barely-put-together jumble of smells and stains that hadn't always been part of my look.

A smile softened his face, and I could see that words had finally come to him. "I salute you…" he said, pausing for a split second to emphasize his next word, "Mother." His sincerity touched me through the busyness that had overtaken me. I blinked hard and smiled. Weary and disheveled, I stood tall, sheathed in the true dignity of motherhood.

— Debra Larson —

My Prayer

Lord, keep me mindful
that the little things I do every day
to raise my children,
I do for you.
Some days are harder than others,
but let me shine with your love
and reflect what is pleasing in your eyes.
Amen.

10

One Last Recital

Listen, my son, to your father's instruction
and do not forsake your mother's teaching.
They will be a garland to grace your head
and a chain to adorn your neck.
~Proverbs 1:8-9

As a child, I often sat at my mother's side on the piano bench while she played or gave me lessons. Sara's small fingers could coax the most beautiful music from a worn-out country school upright or a magnificent Steinway grand. She loved songs from the thirties and forties and hymns, but she was equally at home playing Beethoven and Mozart.

Growing up in the backwoods of Georgia on a red dirt farm near the Chattahoochee River, Mother was the youngest of nine children. She was continually ill from bad tonsils, and old Dr. Chase told her mother he didn't think Sara would live long unless she could get to a hospital and a doctor in the city for a tonsillectomy. Grandma shook her head sadly. There was no money for such things. Even Dr. Chase had to be paid with chickens and eggs. So Grandma did what she knew best. She prayed.

That summer, Sara and her sisters were playing in the barn store-room. A dilapidated old dresser in one corner provided an abundant supply of old clothes for the girls to play dress-up. They arrayed themselves in worn-out lace shirtwaists and flared skirts, tattered straw hats, moth-eaten gloves and purses. Completing their outfits with run-down lace-up boots, they tottered into the house to regale their mother with their finery.

"Look!" said Sara, as she opened her purse with the broken snap and pulled out the pretty papers she had found under the paper liner in the dresser drawer. "I even have play money!"

Her mother's mouth dropped open. "Where did you get these?" she gasped, taking the "play money" from Sara's hand. The "pretty papers" were World War I Liberty Bonds, which an unknown someone had left in the dresser. Cashed in, there was enough money to pay for Sara's tonsillectomy.

The little girl who probably would not have lived grew up to play on a state champion high school basketball team. Mother played the piano and organ for school, church, community events, revival meetings and college songfests. She married and raised three children. She played for our dancing lessons, recitals, church and club functions, family Christmas caroling and birthday parties. Her grandchildren and great-grandchildren sat in her lap while she played and sang for them. She even played on a steam circus calliope that was in a parade.

Mother was eighty-one years old when a fall put her in a halo cast for more than three months. When she was able to sit in a wheelchair, I took her into the hospital rec room. She saw the piano, and her lovely grey, nearly blind eyes lit up. Putting her chair in front of the piano, I sat next to her on a bench as I had so many years ago. Her small arthritic fingers caressed the keys with delight, and she began to play, haltingly at first, and then slowly springing into a lovely medley of her old thirties and forties favorites and hymns.

I couldn't hold back the tears. Suddenly, aware of a rustling behind us, I turned to find a great many of the hospital staff had quietly crept in to listen. Some of them were in tears. Unaware of her audience, Mother played until she tired. The staff gave a huge ovation. God had granted Mom one more recital before she went to be with her Lord a week later.

— Gigi Adam —

My Prayer

Dear Father,
thank you for a mother
whose love spans the generations.
I am grateful for the many lessons
I learned at her side,
and that my children and grandchildren
were blessed to know
and learn from her.
Amen.

11

Jack-in-the-Box Bedtime

Set a guard over my mouth, O LORD;
keep watch over the door of my lips.
~Psalm 141:3

L ike most parents of young children, I looked forward to those precious few moments of household quiet when everyone was tucked into bed. For my first three children, a simple routine of bath, pajamas, and a story had always done the trick. But with my fourth child, a beautiful daughter adopted from China, bedtimes became a new challenge in parenting.

An active five-year-old, my darling girl turned bedtime rituals into a jack-in-the-box experience: I tucked her into bed and went downstairs, and she soon popped out of bed and found my location.

Of course, every appearance she made was accompanied by a request. One night, we had an extra drink, made the inevitable trip to the bathroom, found a special stuffed animal, and cleared out any possible monsters under the bed. Finally, I sent her back without the comfort of an extra tuck-in and with a stern admonition, "If you get out of bed one more time, you will lose outdoor privileges for all of tomorrow." It was the ultimate consequence for her, and I prayed as she went back up the steps, asking for guidance on what to say should she return, with the hope of avoiding a fully pitched battle of the wills.

But she showed up again, and I was forced to make good on my threat. In a calm voice, I said, "You have now lost all outdoor privileges tomorrow. Go back to bed before you lose something else."

Her answer was like a sucker-punch of rage. "My real mother wouldn't make me go back to bed. She loved me!"

It was one of those frozen tableaux. A thousand thoughts went through my head, the foremost of which was a possible answer, one born in frustration. No, your real mother abandoned you and was never heard from again. Fortunately, it wasn't the answer that came out of my mouth. In one of those wonderful Holy Spirit moments, I heard myself say, "Yes, she did love you, but so do I, and I am sending you back to bed. Now."

Her little face with those lovely almond-shaped eyes registered the fact that she was now out of ammunition in the battle of the wills. The fact that she couldn't rattle me by challenging my place in her life seemed to comfort her, and she headed back to bed. I checked later, and she was soundly asleep.

Because I had prayed, that split-second decision between thought and speech ended with the ultimate reassurance to my daughter. It was the difference between comfort and destruction. It's a lesson I've not soon forgotten when it comes to matters of the tongue.

— Deborah L. Kaufman —

My Prayer

Dear Father,
I confess that my thoughts are not your thoughts.
Take control of my speech and
help me to speak the words my children need to hear.
Let my words always be a comfort to them.
Amen.

12

Be Still

> *"Be still, and know that I am God..."*
> *~Psalm 46:10*

Ever have one of those days… weeks… months when your children drain you of every bit of energy you have? As a mom of four, there are many days when I think I just can't handle one more thing. In a span of just a month, I had to rush two of my children to the ER—one for sticking a barrette in her ear and the other with a middle ear infection. The week before, I had another one with a bladder infection and made the appointment for my fourth one with his counselor for anxiety attacks. There is no magic pill for "Worn-Out Mommy Month." That old commercial, "Calgon, take me away," just doesn't cut it. I wanted a limo to come and whisk me away to a five-star hotel with room service. I longed for my world to quit careening out of control.

One night after my husband got home from work, I told him it was absolutely necessary for me to get away for a little bit. Seeing the raving lunatic under the surface, he quickly sent me on my way, and I left for the beach.

One of the blessings of living in Florida is the beach. You walk on the sand and it feels like an instant vacation. I walked to a secluded spot and plopped down on a little hill, close enough to watch the waves come in, but far enough to not get wet. Then I let God have it. I told Him about my awful month. I told Him how unfair it was. Then a scripture popped into my head (not by accident, I'm sure).

"Be still, and know that I am God..." (Psalm 46:10).

Sarcastically, I said, "Okay, I'm being still and knowing you are God."

I folded my arms around my knees and watched the waves. A soothing calm permeated my body as the waves came in and out. I slowly worked out my kinked muscles and overloaded brain. I closed my eyes and relaxed. About that time, I heard a wave that sounded as if it was going to get me all wet. I opened my eyes and saw it was about a foot away. Immediately, God spoke.

"Michelle, you don't trust me."

Huh?

I brushed it off and closed my eyes again. I heard another wave and opened my eyes, afraid that I was fixing to get wet. God spoke to me a second time.

"See, you don't trust me."

True to my stubborn form, I told God that it was just a stupid wave. He informed me that wasn't the point.

Rolling my eyes, I closed them. God told me to listen to the waves. Whenever I heard the froth of a wave bubbling near me, I squeezed my eyes shut, trying not to peek. The next one came, and I relaxed. As each wave came and left without touching me, God began speaking to my heart.

Oftentimes, life can be so loud that we forget to sneak in quiet time. Wave after wave comes, and we feel like we are soaking in frustration and anxiety. I walked away from the beach that day knowing that God would take care of this mother's anxiety and worn-out body. The waves are inevitable, but if am still before Him, He will keep them from overwhelming me.

— Michelle Rocker —

My Prayer

Dear Lord,
when I am overwhelmed,
help me to remain still before you,
knowing that you will provide me with enough
patience to get through the day.
I can do all of this through your constant,
everlasting love.
Amen.

13

Listening for God's Voice

My sheep listen to my voice;
I know them, and they follow me.
~John 10:27

The labor-room nurses wouldn't tell me what was happening. One minute, my husband was counting aloud, pacing my breathing through the contractions and reminding me that soon we'd hold our firstborn child, a daughter. Then, without warning, the room swarmed with people.

"What's happening?" I cried. "Is the baby all right?"

"Just a minute," a nurse answered, her tone brusque. She fit an oxygen mask over my mouth and nose, and flipped me over—the better to get oxygen to the baby, I guessed, but I didn't know for sure. From my position, I couldn't see anything but the headboard of the hospital bed. All I could do was listen, but I heard little in the way of clues. My husband, ordered by a nurse to stand quietly in the corner of the room, had no calm words of encouragement for me. Something was wrong with the baby, and I felt helpless and alone, without a hand to squeeze or a glimpse of the bigger picture.

"God," I prayed, "I don't know what's wrong, but you do. Please help my baby."

I didn't have to wait long after uttering my desperate prayer. A doctor recognized that I was ready to deliver, and at last informed me of what was transpiring. The umbilical cord had twined around the baby's neck, depriving her of oxygen. If I couldn't deliver quickly, I'd have an emergency C-section.

Our daughter was born minutes later, feisty, crying, and healthy. The moment I held her in my arms, I crooned the sorts of words that mothers have murmured to their newborns through the ages—words of welcome, joy, and love. At the sound of my voice, she quieted, and her eyes opened. Her expression smoothed into something akin to relief. I realized then that although she had never seen my face, she knew who I was. She understood that I was her mother, the one who loved her and would do everything I could for her good, even though we'd never gazed upon each other. She recognized me by my voice.

Since that day, there have been several occasions when I have not been able to see the bigger picture, much less God at work in the difficulties I've faced as a parent. Schoolyard bullies, nights in the emergency room, broken hearts, and broken friendships have forced me on my knees, yearning to feel God's arms of comfort and asking for His wisdom. My vision, however, was often obscured, just like it was by the hospital headboard the day my daughter was born.

But then I remember the lesson I learned in that delivery room. Though she had never seen me, my daughter heard my voice and recognized me as the mother who loved and cared for her. In the same way, even when I can't see the bigger picture, God is with me, just as He was the day of my daughter's birth. I recognize Him by His tender love, His gracious care, and His voice.

— Susanne Dietze —

My Prayer

Lord, thank you for guiding us
and never leaving us,
whether or not we can see you at work.
Help us to recognize your voice
even when we can't see the bigger picture.
Let us place our full trust in you.
Amen.

14

Seven Times in a Day

"In your anger do not sin":
Do not let the sun go down while
you are still angry.
~Ephesians 4:26

The shrill cry of the alarm woke me from an uneasy sleep. Despite the softer greeting of the morning songbirds and the promise of sunshine glimmering through the curtains, I was reluctant to get out of bed.

"Duty calls," I muttered, knowing it was time to wake the kids for school. Making my way to the kitchen to start breakfast, I realized my disgruntled mood was the result of still being upset with my ten-year-old son, Michael, from the day before. When was he going to learn to obey me? And why did he make the same mistakes over and over? Nothing seemed to sink in! Glancing at the clock, I knew I'd better start making the rounds to be sure everyone was up.

As I opened the door to Michael's room, his tousled, curly head peeked from beneath the covers. With his oh-so-familiar grin, Michael said, "I'm sorry, Mom. I didn't mean to do it." Always before, his sweet smile had melted my heart. This time, I was determined to teach him a lesson he would not forget.

"Michael, you always say you're sorry. This time, I am not going to forgive you."

As I shut the door, satisfied that I'd followed through on my conviction, I caught a glimpse of his crestfallen face and the disbelief in his eyes.

Walking away, I could not erase the image of Michael's face. "How can you not forgive him?" the Lord whispered in my ear. "Don't you remember what I have said about forgiveness? 'If your brother sins, rebuke him, and if he repents, forgive him. If he sins against you seven times in a day, and seven times comes back to you and says, "I repent," forgive him'" (Luke 17:3-4). God's voice continued, "When you honor my word and obey me, you set the example for Michael."

"But Lord," I argued, "forgiving is not easy, especially when someone keeps on offending."

I stood there struggling with mixed emotions, but then admitted, "I don't like the way this anger is making me feel. Please take it away."

As I felt the feelings of hostility toward Michael slip away, I slowly turned around and headed back to his room. I knew I had to tell him that I forgave him and restore that familiar smile. I also knew I had to ask Michael to forgive me.

— Karen R. Kilby —

My Prayer

Father, encourage me to remember
how many times you forgive me every day.
So many times, I have disappointed you
through my actions,
but you always find it in your heart to forgive.
Help me to follow your pure example.
Amen.

15

Making the Big Decisions

*The seed will grow well, the vine will
yield its fruit, the ground will produce its crops,
and the heavens will drop their dew.
I will give all these things as an inheritance
to the remnant of this people.*
~Zechariah 8:12

I had just dropped my twins off at pre-kindergarten and was standing in the school's parking lot talking with three other mothers of children in my kids' class.

"What public school are you zoned for?" we asked each other.

"Are you going to have your children tested for the gifted program?" another mother asked.

"We might try to get into the dual-language program," one of them said.

"We're looking at private schools," said another.

We went back and forth, comparing the pros and cons of the various schools and programs available for kindergarten.

This was a discussion I'd held with many other parents in the past year. After all, the transition to kindergarten is typically the time when parents have to make the "big decision" as to where their children will go to school. Will they attend a public or private school? A religious school or home school? How about a gifted program? Dual-language? Or a school for the arts?

As I stood in the parking lot that day pondering my choices—and feeling quite overwhelmed by all of the opinions being expressed by the other mothers—I felt pressured. Would my husband and I make the "right" choice for our children? Would they be missing out if we didn't follow the crowd or enroll them in an expensive school? The choice weighed heavily on my mind as I got into the car to go home.

Suddenly, I realized this wasn't a decision my husband and I had to make alone. As with any of the "big decisions" in life, we could ask God for guidance in finding the answer we sought. I felt a weight lift from my heart and did my best to put my worries aside. In the weeks and months ahead, my husband and I continued to seek advice from other parents, as well as our children's current teacher, but we also sought counsel from within, where God's steady presence dwells.

My boys are now thriving in kindergarten. Their teachers fit their personalities perfectly, and I really felt God's hand at work in guiding us in this decision. Ironically, we didn't choose the same school as any of the mothers who were in the parking lot with me that day. But we still keep in touch, and I know that they are happy with their choices, just as we are happy with ours. With a Christ-centered approach to decision-making, we figured out what was best for our family and our children's needs.

— Susan M. Heim —

My Prayer

*Lord, please guide me in listening to your counsel
when it comes to making the "big decisions"
in my family's life. I know that you are totally
accessible to us whenever we are in need.
Help me to recognize your voice.
Amen.*

Love in a JCPenney Catalog

And now these three remain: faith, hope and love.
But the greatest of these is love.
~1 Corinthians 13:13

I scanned the pages of the JCPenney catalog as our children slept. My husband was working the night shift, and this was the only way I could finish my Christmas shopping. I checked off items on each child's wish list. I tried not to think about how much I was about to add to my charge card. I flipped through the pages of children's clothing and drifted to the toy section to pick out a few items.

Ron and I had been married five years. Our blended family included his two girls, my four boys, and our toddler son. We both worked hard to provide a home for our children, but the past year had been clouded with arguments and resentment. Everyone in the family was adjusting to the challenges that so many blended families experience, including alimony, child support, and shared weekends. Each one of these challenges seemed to lead to a new argument, and I was having a difficult time pretending to be joyous about the Christmas season.

I let out a sigh and thought back to a day, five years earlier, when Ron and I had gone to marriage counseling.

"The average blended family takes five to seven years to gel," said the counselor.

"Hmmm," I mumbled.

"That is, if your marriage lasts that long. And only if you both have the support of your ex-spouses."

I glanced over at Ron. Oh, boy. Five years? Who has that kind of patience?

Ron took my hand. "What we need is the six-month plan, Doc," he said. "That's why we're here. We have seven children depending on us. This needs to work now, not five years from now."

She stared back at us. "I see. Well, good luck to both of you."

Five years had passed since that counseling session, and I had lost my enthusiasm for this marriage. Darn, she was right, I thought.

I thought about a recent argument with my stepdaughter that had escalated to an all-out screaming match. I had tried to be the perfect mother, stepmother, and wife, but I had been falling short of that goal for many months.

I flipped to the back of the catalog. On page 758, my eyes were immediately drawn to a wall tapestry with the same dusty rose and green colors of my bedroom. I reached over to the nightstand and grabbed my reading glasses. I leaned in closer to the page. My heart raced as I read the words from 1 Corinthians 13 in the center of the tapestry:

"Love is patient and kind, love is not jealous or boastful; it is not arrogant or rude."

I remember these words, I thought.

"Love does not insist on its own way; it is not irritable or resentful."

I took a deep breath and read further.

"It does not rejoice at wrong, but rejoices in the right. Love bears all things, believes all things, hopes all things, endures all things."

My chin dropped to my chest, and tears ran down my cheek. Finally, I started giggling.

"Sending your love through a JCPenney catalog? Well, God, that's different!" I laughed as I glanced up.

I ordered clothes and toys for the children for Christmas—and the tapestry for our room.

Ten years have passed since that evening, and the tapestry still hangs on a wall in our bedroom. It is a constant reminder of God's unfailing love and our unconditional love for one another. We have had our challenges, but we continue to grow stronger in our love and respect for each other. We count our blessings, and we continue to believe, hope, and endure all things together. We are a family.

— Meagan Greene Friberg —

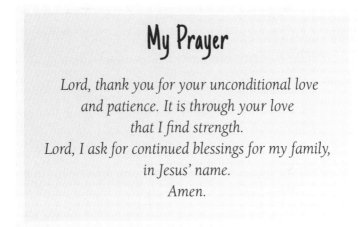

My Prayer

Lord, thank you for your unconditional love
and patience. It is through your love
that I find strength.
Lord, I ask for continued blessings for my family,
in Jesus' name.
Amen.

17

God's Wake-Up Call

The Sovereign LORD has given me an instructed
tongue, to know the word that sustains the weary.
He wakens me morning by morning,
wakens my ear to listen like one being taught.
~Isaiah 50:4

I hear a faint song playing in the background. It's Michael W. Smith singing "Awesome God." The song repeats, again and yet again. If you've ever had a song stuck in your head, you know how annoying it can be! I mean no disrespect for one of God's great songs. It's just that the song is playing over and over in my head at 2:30 in the morning. So, I do the only thing I can do—get up.

I chuckle as my feet hit the carpet and think, "All right, all right, I'm up!" Some people might continue to brood between the sheets or fall back to sleep, but I can't. I know the routine. The song will be relentlessly played, not by the radio, but by God. This is God's bat phone, and when it rings, I have to get up to answer it.

This started when my firstborn son was a year old. I had started going to my first Bible study for women as one of my only adult out-ings as a stay-at-home mom. I treasured the time with the women, but it grew into something more than a few "me moments." I came to savor the time I sporadically found to connect with God during my half-hearted, interrupted attempts to do my study and connect with God at home. The Word of God was a spark flickering in the depths of my cold heart, and I desperately needed to fan the flame to get a fire going. But things would creep in to fill the day to the point of exhaustion. I was frustrated and weary, but determined.

So, I set my alarm for 6:00 a.m. to have some time with God. That lasted about two days until my son started waking up at 6:00. Still determined, I set my alarm to get up at 5:00 a.m. You can probably guess what happened. Within the week, my son started waking up around 5:00. I was ticked off! I could clearly see that the enemy was blocking my time with God and using my own son to do it! I couldn't get up any earlier, so I had to figure out something else.

Then God and the angels had a meeting, and God said, "Hey, I've got a good one. Why don't I drive her nuts with some song in her head to wake her up? She'll have to get up and connect with me!" And so it was. I quickly figured out that God has a quirky sense of humor, and this was His way of connecting with me.

As moms, it can be difficult to carve out time for ourselves and God. Sometimes, we have to do things in creative ways to accomplish all that needs to be done. Thankfully, God has some great ideas for connecting!

— Renee Crosby —

My Prayer

I thank you, Father,
for being a God who seeks us out.
I pray that mothers everywhere
will strive to find time to connect with you,
and to be responsive to the cues you so freely give.
Amen.

18

Without Conditions

*...I pray that you, being rooted and established
in love, may have power, together with all the saints,
to grasp how wide and long and high and deep is the
love of Christ, and to know this love that surpasses
knowledge — that you may be filled to the measure
of all the fullness of God.*
~Ephesians 3:17-19

The doctor walked in with a twinkle in his eye. "Well, Linda, you're pregnant."

My nine-month-old son, Rob, squirmed in my lap in an effort to get on the office floor.

Another baby?

After making an appointment for the next month I went home to give the good news to my husband and three-year-old daughter. Since I still had a baby boy, I secretly hoped for another girl so I could dress her in bows and lace. For nine months, I nurtured this hope.

But God's plan is always higher than mine, and this child would come with a message.

In the delivery room, the doctor announced, "It's a boy!" My heart sank a little. But when they placed Charles in my arms, I regretted every second I had wasted wanting a girl.

All too soon, he was whisked away to the nursery, with the promise that he'd be back for his next feeding. That evening, I heard him wailing in the hall as the nurse brought him to me. I took my crying, red-faced son, and soon he calmed down enough to nurse. We studied each other's faces.

You know that feeling when love wells up so big inside you that it makes it hard to breathe? That's what I felt.

He finished and burped all over my shoulder, then made a dirty diaper. I changed and swaddled him, and then watched my newborn drift off to sleep. His face was now a peaceful pink.

Guilt still nagged at me. Oh, how could I have ever been disappointed? At that moment, I sensed the Lord asking me, "Do you love Charles?"

My answer was immediate. "Oh, yes. I love him so much it hurts."

"Why do you love him? What has he done to earn your love?"

Actually, he hadn't done anything to earn my love. He couldn't. He came into the room demanding to be fed. Then he made a mess. And he didn't even muster up a gas smile of appreciation for his meal before he fell asleep.

Still, I loved him so much it almost took my breath away.

"Lord, he hasn't done anything to earn my love. But I love him because he's my son. He doesn't have to earn it."

"That, my child, is how I love you—without conditions. I love you even when you are demanding, messy, and ungrateful."

All of a sudden, I realized the kind of relationship God wanted to have with all His children. Holding my sleeping babe, I wept at the enormity of this message. He loved me because I was His.

In fact, He loved me so much it hurt.

— Linda Apple —

My Prayer

Lord, thank you for loving me
in spite of my imperfection and weakness.
Help me to respond to and accept
your unconditional love.
Amen.

19

One of Life's Greatest Blessings

*Cast your cares on the LORD and he will
sustain you; he will never let the righteous fall.*
~Psalm 55:22

I think all little girls dream about being a mother. I did. I wanted to be the best mommy ever. But I came to mothering in an unusual way.

During my last year of law school, my sister was facing drug charges. She had battled drugs for years, and it took its toll on her three children, the youngest of whom was just turning eleven. When my sister was no longer able to care for her youngest child, my heart began to urge me. Sure, I would be there for Ami. I was always there for Ami, and I would still be there for Ami. But at that point, what that meant was really not defined for me. What did God want from me?

It became defined over the next several months as my sister fled the country, leaving Ami behind. Someone needed to fill in the gap. I was young. I had no children of my own. I had my life ahead of me and a promising career. I had prospective suitors. I did not need a child to complicate my life or my future. But a still small voice kept urging me on.

"Take in Ami."

"You are what she needs."

"I will give you what you need."

"I will sustain you."

Still, none of it was enough for me to make the final decision.

Friends would tell me, "It will ruin your life. Taking Ami will interfere with your future and hamper your prospects of marriage and children." But then the clear and gentle whisper of the Lord would come to my ear. It shook my very being to the core, and I knew that the Lord wanted me to take in this child and raise her as my own.

So, I did just that. I formed my family around an angry, bitter eleven-year-old child who was hurt immensely by all that had happened to her. And it wasn't easy. In fact, it was downright hard to do on my own as a single parent. But His promises were true. I was what Ami needed, and the Lord gave me everything I needed. He was with me every step of the way. He helped me and sustained me through it all with many joys and laughs.

I sometimes ponder what my life would have been like without Ami. I would have missed out on one of life's greatest blessings if I had not been obedient to the Lord's calling. I have a beautiful, smart, talented daughter who has brought great joy to my life. Although she chased away many of my beaux during her growing-up years, she could not scare off my reward. I see my husband today as God's reward to me for listening to His voice and being obedient to His call. Matt is a wonderful, loving man who embraced Ami where she was and shares my heart for the orphan.

Ami graduated college with a degree in Communications and a minor in Biology. She teaches science to at-risk students. She is very popular among her students, who relate well to her. She has the talent to reach children whom others cannot reach and to encourage them beyond their circumstances to something better.

After raising Ami, I realized that if given another opportunity, I would gladly do it all again in spite of the challenges I faced. I didn't realize the opportunity would arrive so quickly. My husband and I signed up for foster parenting classes shortly after Ami graduated. Her letter of recommendation was all it took for us to be on to our next divine appointment.

— Clara Cooper —

My Prayer

Lord, continue to use me as a mother
for the many needy children of this world.
It is through your lessons of love
that I learn to open up my heart.
May I always have these opportunities
to serve you.
Amen.

20

Time for Myself

"In repentance and rest is your salvation,
in quietness and trust is your strength..."
~Isaiah 30:15

My husband and I both work from home. We have four children, so the times when I am alone in the house are few and far between. Like many work-at-home moms, when I do get a chance to be by myself, I fill that time with more work, whether it's related to my career or taking care of the household chores. Most of the time, I don't mind. After all, I wanted this "gig" as wife and mother, and I knew from the start that it often entailed putting others' needs before my own. But, other times, I can't help but feel a little resentful.

One day, things really came to a head. My husband was heading out to the gym, just assuming I had nothing to do but watch the twins. My older boys were making plans with their friends without consulting me — plans that involved having me drive them quite a distance from home. The twins, being young, wanted my undivided attention. Even my work clients seemed to be more demanding that day. Nobody bothered to ask if I might have plans of my own. But, the truth was, I rarely did have any plans for myself, and everyone knew it. My life revolved around them, and they took advantage of that.

The next day, when the kids were at school, I headed for the movie theater—alone. I'd never been to the movies alone before, so I was a little nervous. Would I look pitiful going to the theater by myself? Was I being frivolous by seeing a movie when so much work awaited me at home? I forced myself to swallow these thoughts and buy myself a ticket. And then I walked into the theater with my head held high and enjoyed every minute of the movie. I laughed and felt my good spirits return. For a couple of hours, I was nobody's wife or mother. I was just myself.

From that point on, I decided that Fridays would be mine, at least for a couple of hours. Some Fridays, I head to the beach with a good book. Other Fridays, I go shopping and indulge in a little "retail therapy." I may pick up a little fast food or a gourmet coffee just for myself. I really look forward to my Fridays after a long week of caring for my family.

By forcing myself to slow down and put the needs of my family out of my mind (well, almost), I also feel closer to my Creator. Sitting alone on the beach, I'm not focused on the children's safety around the water. I'm drinking in God's majesty and feeling his Spirit in the air and the waves around me. Even at the theater, I think about what God might be trying to teach me through the story I'm seeing. When I buy myself a yummy treat, I thank God for being able to savor His bounty and for always providing for my needs. I realize that I'm not solely responsible for caring for my family. God is taking care of all of us; I don't need to do it all myself. And He is taking care of me when I'm feeling overwhelmed or overburdened. I just need to remember to carve out time to be with Him—alone.

— Susan M. Heim —

My Prayer

Dear Father,
I thank you for the gift of being a wife and mother.
I know that all of us were created equal,
and you are here to meet all of our needs—
even my own.
Help me to remember that your love for me
is ever present.
Amen.

21

One of Those Days

...The LORD is the everlasting God, the Creator of the ends of the earth. He will not grow tired or weary, and his understanding no one can fathom. He gives strength to the weary and increases the power of the weak.
~Isaiah 40:28-29

It was one of those days.

I'd been cooped up in the house with two kids, had a work deadline, and could feel a sinus infection coming on.

The day had started pretty well. That morning, I was cuddling in bed with seven-year-old Jordan and two-year-old Jackson. Jordan said, "Jackson is so cute, I could die!"

Contented sigh.

But it was all downhill from there. Later that day, Jordan and Jax were playing with markers. At one point, I noticed that Jordan had scribbled "kick me" on Jax's lower back above his diaper. I had to laugh, but I also had to work at getting the marker off with an unscheduled bath.

As for the newly tattooed toddler, his day was spent screaming at the top of his lungs and taking off his diaper.

By two o'clock, I was ready to run out the door screaming. When the baby's naptime finally came, I tried to work, but then I realized that this was one of those times when I just needed to be still.

And so I was.

Turning off the computer, I poured myself a cup of tea, sat in my favorite chair and opened my journal.

With a smile, I saw that my life hadn't changed much in the past few months. One entry read: "Jordan brought me two dead crickets, a fake fingernail, and (oh, yes!) some crumpled rose petals from the bush in the backyard." As I kept reading about my little boys' antics, I started to chuckle. Hey, I thought, I don't need sitcoms or the funny papers. I have two boys!

Continuing in a quiet—and slowly improving—mood, I opened the scriptures.

The book of Isaiah is a particular favorite when I'm feeling insecure, frustrated or unsure. Once again, I was comforted and encouraged by the Word, and by being in God's presence.

I didn't hear any audible voices or bells ringing, but as I told my husband later, "The crazies went away." I was able to regain my equilibrium and realize that it's okay to feel nuts once in a while. God loves me anyway.

Contented sigh.

Those moments of grace in the midst of mommyhood help me remember that each day, with God's strength, I'm doing the best I can in the roles I've been given.

And that's enough.

I need those times with my Maker to remind me that my boys are not burdens—they are my biggest blessings! In the midst of Crazyville, He helps me keep my perspective—and a sense of humor.

— Dena Dyer —

My Prayer

Lord, help me remember to make time for stillness
in the midst of my busy days.
Thank you for the calm that comes
when I center my thoughts on you
and allow you to quiet my soul.
Amen.

22

P.S. Pray

I waited patiently for the LORD;
he turned to me and heard my cry.
~Psalm 40:1

Dear Son,

We all miss you. My heart aches with the choices that led you down this awful road that ended in a detention facility. I would do anything to fix your life for you, but I know that only you and the Lord can do that. I pray that your time in there will help you understand that real happiness can only come from doing what is right. Please know that we love you and are praying for you.

Love, Mom

P.S. Pray.

My tears blurred the words on the page before me. In all honesty, I didn't know what to say, didn't know how to fix things. The mother in me just wanted to make it all better, but I knew this was something I couldn't fix. My sixteen-year-old son would have to do this on his own, with God's forgiveness and help.

Exhaustion became normal as deep-rooted anxiety kept me agonizing and praying for my child. He was so lost. With big blue-green eyes filled with mischief and humor, my thoughtful, kind little boy grew to be a teenager I never dreamed he would be. His choices brought him to a darker and darker way of living. I watched as he changed before my eyes, becoming unhappy and angry, and spiraling steadily downward. It was tearing our family apart and my heart to shreds. Now the only way I could reach him was through occasional visits and mail, which they allowed him to read, then took away.

Each day, I began a new letter, tucking it into a card with a funny joke or a spiritual message. I prayed hard to know what to say, to know what my Father would have me tell my son that would make a difference. With each letter, I felt inadequate in my words, but I always ended with the same postscript: "P.S. Pray."

I received one letter from my son while he was incarcerated.

Dear Mom,

I am so sorry for all the things I've done. I miss you all so much, and I can't wait to get out of here to start over. I love you so much. I'm reading my scriptures every day, and I think this has been good for me. I needed to be here. I can't wait to come home.

P.S. I'm praying.

When my son came home, he had a new light in his eyes. He seemed focused, happy, and appreciative. We welcomed him with open arms, and soon his life was back on track.

One day, we were talking about his time in detention. I asked him what it was like, and he said it was part hell and part heaven. I asked him how it could ever be like heaven, and he said that with nothing to do but read scripture and pray, it had brought him closer to God than at any other time in his life. He told me how my letters made him homesick, but he always looked for my little postscript, which was like his compass.

We take it day by day now. We end each day with prayer as a family. My son has so much potential to be a great man who walks with the Lord. He still makes mistakes, but one thing is constant throughout his life: He prays.

— Susan Farr-Fahncke —

My Prayer

Dear Father in heaven, please walk with my child
and never let him forget he belongs to you.
Guide and protect him in every moment
of every day, and remind him that you cherish him
and forgive him.
He needs you.
Amen.

23

A Letting-Go Kind of Love

The LORD is close to the brokenhearted
and saves those who are crushed in spirit.
~Psalm 34:18

He didn't want to tell me, afraid I'd march back to the school with a shaking finger and motherly lecture for a few of his peers. But I pressed. And pressed. After all, I'm a mom who makes an art out of extracting important information. Weary of my relentless questions, he finally confessed.

"Some kids have been picking on me at school."

Ah, the reason he'd been quiet. I kept my mouth shut, afraid any sound would stifle his transparency. Instead, I nodded my encouragement to continue.

"It happens mostly in Spanish, but sometimes in other classes and on the bus."

He described several incidents, nothing ruthless or dangerous, but not particularly enjoyable either. Most of the kids involved were kids we'd known for years. Then my son scrunched up his face and shrugged, unwilling to give vent to the emotions lurking below the surface.

"I don't really care, I guess. But it gets old."

I could tell he cared more than he let on, and the mother bear in me wanted to shoot off a scathing e-mail to his teachers or drive straight to the school office, educate them on the dangers of bullying, and demand an intervention. As if reading my thoughts, he begged, "Don't say anything, Mom. Please. It'll just make things worse. I can handle it."

The lines on his young face and the intensity in his eyes made me doubt it. I could see his hurt, and my heart nearly broke as a result.

"I'm sorry, sweetheart. What these kids are doing... well, it's not right." He shrugged again.

I gave him a hug, told him I loved him and was so proud of him, and then released him to his homework. After he left, I sat at my desk, head in my hands and ready to cry. Is there anything worse than the helpless moments of motherhood?

When he was a baby and cried from hunger, I fed him. When he needed a clean diaper, I changed him. Any time he cut a finger or scratched a knee, I ran to the rescue with Band-Aids and peroxide, ready to fix whatever was broken.

But I couldn't fix this brokenness. I'd respect his request and not intervene — yet. Being a middle-school boy was tough enough without a pushy, overbearing mother. I'd have to sit back and watch him wrestle through this challenge, praying he'd rise above it, stronger and more mature as a result.

It was then that I got a glimpse of God's role in parenting me. At times, He's come to my rescue, diving in to pluck me from the middle of a struggle. Other times, He's allowed me to wrestle through the difficulty, hoping I'd grow and mature in the process. Occasionally, I've wondered if God is callous, unconcerned with my pain. But as I sat at my desk with my heart bleeding for my son, I understood that sometimes parenting means not intervening. It's learning to love by letting go, allowing your own heart to break in order to allow them to live their own story. And then waiting to hold them when they need a safe place in which to fall.

— Michele Cushatt —

My Prayer

Father, help me to learn
when to intervene and when to let go.
Help me to trust that your love for my children
is even greater than mine.
Even in times of uncertainty,
you are there to help heal the situation.
Amen.

24

Over the Rainbow

"For I know the plans I have for you,"
declares the LORD, "plans to prosper you
and not to harm you, plans to give
you hope and a future."
~Jeremiah 29:11

My daughter clasped my hand and said, "It's okay, Mom. It's time!" Tears rolled down my face as I marveled at my daughter's courage. After twenty-four hours of labor, little Kailee was born. The doctor placed the squalling baby in my daughter's arms. She softly touched the brow of her newborn and said, "Shhh, honey. It's okay. Don't cry!"

For three days, the nurses brought Kailee to be fed and changed. It would have been wonderful, except Kailee would be placed in another mother's arms within days. As I held Kailee, my body trembled. I did not want to see her go! Standing by my daughter's bedside, old clichés came to mind: "Give it time," or "Lean on God!" Both were true statements, but my daughter needed more than clichés. So did I.

Two days later, when the social worker arrived, I knew the moment for Kailee's departure was near. In the tiny hospital room, our family held hands and prayed together. "Dear Lord, please be near Sarah and help her to understand that adoption was the right decision. And help Kailee to grow in your love. May the day come when we can be reunited."

After Kailee left the room in the arms of the social worker, silence prevailed. "We'll get through this together, honey," I said to my daughter. We gathered the cards, balloons and presents, and I pushed Sarah in a wheelchair to the lobby. My husband left to bring our car to the entrance. Sarah looked up at me and said, "Mom, I can't believe it. I just gave away my baby!"

I hugged her and uttered yet another cliché. "God must have a great plan!"

As her father arrived, he stretched out his arms and said, "Come on, honey. Lean on me!"

When we arrived home, Sarah went to her room and placed one of her gifts—a music box with a red rose inside—on her shelf. As she wound it, it began to play "Over the Rainbow." But as I listened, the beautiful skies and blue birds seemed very far away.

Eighteen years later, Sarah opened her mail and found a large yellow envelope. Inside were pictures and a letter from Kailee. Tears of joy filled her heart. She telephoned me and yelled, "Mom, you'll never believe it. Kailee wants to meet us!"

Kailee and her adopted family traveled to our little mountain home, and our families were reunited. Questions poured out, such as: "Do you sing?" Sarah grew up singing in church and traveling with a small singing group. Kailee sang in a group, too. Someone asked Sarah if she would sing, and she grabbed a microphone while my husband popped her favorite song into the player. In our small front room, Sarah sang, "God Will Make a Way," by Janet Paschal. We all held hands and cried. Only this time, the tears were filled with happiness.

When the little music box tinkled away one sad afternoon so many years ago, we didn't know the skies would really turn blue and the sun would shine a little bit brighter. Sarah turned to me and smiled, and I knew that God had filled that huge spot deep in her heart.

— Shirley Anne Reynolds —

My Prayer

Lord, help us to remember
that when life seems tough,
and there don't seem to be blue skies and rainbows,
we are walking with you.
You will always provide a purpose for our life.
You alone will give us hope for tomorrow.
Amen.

25

A Real Mother

*"For whoever does the will of my Father in heaven
is my brother and sister and mother."*
~Matthew 12:50

"**I** don't have to mind you," Josh screamed as he swung a brown fist toward my chest. "You're not my real mother." I jumped back, but not far enough. My physical pain would dissipate in a few days, but the pain of not being his "real" mother would continue. I loved Josh, but he showed no affection or respect for anyone, not even me, his foster mother.

Josh had lived with his mother and maternal grandmother in an apartment attached to a tavern. His father left when Josh was a baby. His grandmother cared for him until she died when Josh was four years old. The bar, the only home he had known, closed. He and his mother were homeless. They lived an unsettled life. His mother left him with friends or family and disappeared for days, sometimes weeks, then reappeared again to move in with someone else. She and Josh were staying in a home when a child-endangerment crime was investigated. That's when Josh was brought to my home.

Josh swung at me again. He was small, but strong. Anger had intensified his strength so that his forty-two pounds had downed a student twice his size on the school playground. Now, here he stood, defying me. As Josh screamed his "you-are-not-my-real mother" speech, he exploded, lashing out at me.

"Josh, do you know what a real mother is?" I demanded.

"Whaddaya think? I'm stupid or somethin'?" Josh sneered, then screamed obscenities at me. "My real mother is the one I was born to."

I took a deep breath and launched into my own tirade. "A 'real mother' isn't always the one who gave life to you." I took a chance and moved closer. I looked into his deep brown eyes and lowered my voice. "Josh, a real mother prepares your meals so you won't be hungry. She sends you to school in the mornings and makes sure you do your homework in the evenings. She washes your clothes. At bedtime, she listens to your prayers, reads to you or sings you to sleep. That's a real mother."

Josh turned away and pretended not to hear me. My speech made little difference in his attitude or behavior. He continued to lash out at me.

A few weeks later, Billy, another seven-year-old boy, became a part of our home. He screamed at me, "I don't have to mind you; you're not my real mother." He lacked Josh's speed, so I managed to sidestep or control most of his outbursts without danger to myself, but I questioned my mother role. "I've never birthed a child. What made me think I could make a difference in a neglected child's life?"

Before I could give Billy my well-rehearsed speech about mothers, Josh took him by the hand and led him outside. I watched them through the front window as they wriggled up onto the large front porch swing. Their legs dangled above the wooden plank floor. Josh placed his arm around Billy. I eased the door open and listened as Josh spoke.

"Do you know what a real mother is? She isn't always your birth mother...."

— Violet Carr Moore —

My Prayer

*Heavenly Father, thank you for using me to mother
the lost, lonely and needy children of the world.
You knew this divine plan for my life,
and I ask for the strength, courage and love
to shape the lives of these children.
Amen.*

26

Hug 'Em and Pray

Let us then approach the throne of grace with confidence, so that we may receive mercy and find grace to help us in our time of need.
~Hebrews 4:16

"**M**a'am, your son is in danger of being expelled." I listen as the Dean of Students expounds on my stepson's seventh-grade hallway misadventures, which bring me to the school at least once a week.

My stepson slouches in his chair, and my heart squeezes at the blank look in his eyes. Where is he? Surely he knows that to be accused of stealing is no small matter. Do I believe everything the Dean tells me, which comes from various sources, or trust everything my son says?

My mom would say there are always three sides to every story: this side, that side, and the truth. Only God knows all three sides. I wish God would share.

As difficult as our beginning together was, I love Taylor. I do not understand him. Ever. We have been in this no-man's-land of step-relationships since he was nearly three years old. Now thirteen, he calls me Mom, having gotten his own mom's blessing before taking that step. We both work hard to maintain a strong, healthy relationship for his sake, and she is a supportive person in our lives. Like a true mom, she seems to know what to do and say at all times.

Oh, that I could be a real mom.

Taylor does not remember a time when I was not part of his life, but sometimes I wonder if he wishes differently. He would never say so. He is often kind, generous, and loving, but there are times when he withdraws and becomes sullen. His bright countenance turns dark, a stranger I don't recognize. Is it the age, or is something more sinister happening?

He is a stranger now. What is he thinking? What would his mom say? I should call her for advice.

Or should I? Isn't this something his dad and I should fix with him? Just where do we draw the line between parents and stepparents? Moms and stepmoms? Of course, I'll call her about the situation, but maybe I should also back away and stop trying to be a mother.

But then I remember who to ask for advice. God is the ultimate parent, a loving presence in spite of our constant backsliding. He can help me reach Taylor and fight the darkness in his eyes.

"Lord, what do I say? What would you say to him?"

My thoughts go back briefly to a small piece of advice our pastor gave us in premarital counseling ten years ago. "When in doubt," he said, "hug 'em and pray."

Taylor sits quietly on the ride home, and I know I must try to offer the comfort God wants to give him. Reaching over, I squeeze his hand. "I love you."

His tough exterior crumbles. Covering his face with one large hand, his voice cracks. "I love you, too."

This time, I know it will be okay. Whatever we muddle through, we'll do it together, with God. Maybe that's what being a real mom is all about.

— Shelley Ring —

My Prayer

Dear Lord, please help my child and me
to work out our differences, to communicate better,
and to grow in love for one another.
May we always see each other
as perfect creations of you.
Thank you for being the example
we can always look to for help.
Amen.

27

Gold Medals and Tea Kettles

Folly is bound up in the heart of a child,
but the rod of discipline will drive it far from him.
~Proverbs 22:15

I t was 12:30 a.m., and my seventeen-year-old daughter was not home. On a school night. I sat huddled beside my kitchen stove, drinking tea, reading a book, and trying not to worry on this chilly autumn night. At 1:00, she walked in the back door without excuses, and I grounded her for missing her curfew. The next day, I received a card from her with a long, handwritten note inside. My mind immediately went back three or four years to similar times when I'd received scathing, defensive notes pleading her case and telling me how unfair I was.

"Not this again," I thought. "I'm not sure I'm up to it." I took a deep breath, prayed a quick prayer, and read. What unfolded before my eyes turned out to be an absolute treasure! I couldn't have been prouder if they'd hung an Olympic gold medal around my neck. Among other things, she'd written:

"I sincerely regret it. And I'm not just saying I regret being caught, either. I regret scaring you, and I regret being so foolish. So, I sincerely apologize for disobeying you and for any unnecessary stress that I caused, and I ask for your forgiveness.... I respect your grounding me, too. I know discipline isn't exactly the easiest part of raising kids, and I'm sorry for making you do that. I love you."

She even closed with a slightly revised Bible verse: "Raise your child in the way she should go, and when she is old, she will not turn from it" (Proverbs 22:6). Wow! It couldn't get any better than that. I realized she was really growing up, and I loved the young woman she was turning out to be.

Over the years, through the pleading, prayers and tears, I have often been granted a new picture of God. Always the perfect parent, He chose to give us our own free will, even though He could have simply programmed us to obey. I think I'm beginning to understand why. I can no sooner "make" my children obey than I can make them fly. I can make my expectations known and put consequences in place, but the rest is up to them. When they choose to respond in the way that every parent hopes they will, the thrill of victory vastly outweighs the agony of defeat. May that understanding motivate me to obey my Heavenly Father quickly and to run to Him with regret when I've blown it.

I know that neither my daughter nor I have "arrived" yet. We are two very imperfect human beings with selfish hearts and stubborn tendencies. But for today, I'll clutch her letter to my heart like a gold medal around my neck. And when someone asks, "Is it worth it?" I'll respond with a resounding "Yes!"

— Terrie Todd —

My Prayer

Lord, thank you for creating us with a free will.
Please grant me wisdom, courage, and perseverance
when it comes to disciplining my children.
And give me the energy I need
when I have to wait up past curfew!
Amen.

28

Kindred Spirits

This is what the LORD says:
"Restrain your voice from weeping
and your eyes from tears,
for your work will be rewarded,"
declares the LORD. "They will return from
the land of the enemy. So there is hope
for your future," declares the LORD.
"Your children will return to
their own land."
~Jeremiah 31:16-17

The dog stood beside the road, her head moving like a pendulum, watching car after car whip by. At the first break in traffic, her head stopped moving, and her gaze fixed on something lying in the road. Another passing car blocked her tentative step toward the object. Again, she ventured onto the road, and again a car stopped her progress.

I spied what held the mama dog's attention—a lifeless puppy lying in the far lane of the road. "Oh my gosh, that's me," I said aloud. I burst into tears as I recognized the parallel of my attempts to rescue my wounded, drug-addicted son, Isaac. I heard the Holy Spirit whisper, "I see you running back and forth, desperate to reach your son."

Watching the frantic dog, I wondered how many times I had dodged logic and reason in attempting to rescue my son. How many tears had fallen as I waited for him to beat the addiction holding our family hostage? How many times had I done everything I could to avoid walking away from him in despair? My answer rang clearly: countless.

As a mother, I cling to every thread of hope that keeps my child alive for one more day. I start each day with a prayer: "Let today be the day he is set free." The urge to give up on my son often outweighs the desire to stand and fight one more battle. The temptation to speak sharply, or not at all, looms large when confronted with another lie. The disgust I feel when another item goes missing jerks me back to the reality of his addiction. I cannot leave him in the road; he is alive. And with life, there is hope.

Children stumble and fall whether they are toddlers, teenagers or adults. Mothers instinctively know how and when to kiss their children's scraped places and send them back into the world. The scraped knees of childhood sometimes evolve into broken hearts and shattered dreams in adulthood, much harder to soothe away. But the promise in Jeremiah 31:16-17 sustains me when the stumbles outnumber the successful sendoffs.

The dog left her puppy alone in the road, but I will not leave my son. I continue to care and seek God on his behalf. After all, that's what mothers do.

— Sharron K. Cosby —

My Prayer

Dear Father, thank you for the privilege
of being Mom to your precious creations.
Thank you for their stumbles because they lead me
to your throne of grace and mercy.
Thank you for the promise
that my "children will return to their own land"
and my "work will be rewarded."
Amen.

29

Parenting Through Good Times and Bad

*But he said to me, "My grace is sufficient
for you, for my power is made perfect
in weakness." Therefore I will boast
all the more gladly about my weaknesses,
so that Christ's power may rest on me.
That is why, for Christ's sake,
I delight in weaknesses, in insults,
in hardships, in persecutions, in difficulties.
For when I am weak, then I am strong.*
~2 Corinthians 12:9-10

One day while making supper, I watched our four children play-ing. Smiling, I remembered how God had answered our prayers and brought two-year-old Matt into our family. My smile faded as Matt grabbed a car out of Andy's hand. When Andy snatched it back, Matt started crying. No one knew I had been watching.

"What's wrong, Matt?" I asked.

"Andy stole my car," he replied, tears streaming down his face.

"Who had the car first?"

"I did," said Matt, still crying.

The other children sat with mouths agape, shocked at Matt's audacity.

"Matt, I saw Andy with that car before you had it. Please give it back, and then come and talk to me," I said. After explaining that he had told me something untrue—a lie—I gave him a consequence.

My husband and I worked hard at being consistent and fair with our children. Like most parents, we learned through trial and error. We discovered that different children respond differently to the same consequence. Before Matt joined our family, we had stocked our parenting toolbox with a variety of effective tools. The only problem was that Matt did not respond to any of them. He said all the right words—"I'm sorry. I won't do it again. I promise"—but his behavior became worse. One day, our daughter came to me in tears. "Mom, Matt just went upstairs, pulled down his pants, and peed on my stuffed animals."

Matt underwent psychological testing, participated in play therapy, and had a behavior consultant who worked with him at school. Each professional we saw told us we were doing all the right things.

One day, six-year-old Matt stood looking up at me with his defiant chocolate-brown eyes. I gritted my teeth, squelching the desire to yell, throw something or even punch. Matt had lied to me again, but insisted he was telling the truth. I had reached my breaking point. I had done everything I could to reach Matt, but I felt like a failure. I was out of ideas, out of energy, out of hope. God's Spirit, in his gentle, quiet way, spoke to my heart. "My grace is sufficient for you, for my power is made perfect in weakness" (2 Corinthians 12:9). That day, I told God He would have to love Matt through me. I then made a commitment, choosing to love Matt always, even if Matt's behavior never changed.

Two years later, there are still challenging days. Thankfully, I see a little glimmer of hope occasionally. The other day, our children were sharing their middle names.

"What's your middle name, Matt?"

"Samuel."

"That's right. Do you know what it means?" I asked.

"Nope."

"It means 'asked of God.' Mommy and Daddy prayed and asked God for a son."

"And that would be me," Matt replied, with a twinkle in his eye.

"Yes, that would be you," I said with a smile. "And we are glad God answered our prayers by sending you."

— Ruth L. Snyder —

My Prayer

*Dear loving Father, thank you for
knowing the areas in which I struggle as a mother.
Help me to allow you to parent through me,
using my weaknesses for your glory.
Amen.*

30

My Son, My Hero

*In my distress I called to the LORD; I cried to
my God for help. From his temple he heard my voice;
my cry came before him, into his ears.*
~Psalm 18:6

"Erik! I need you. Come grab the baby!" My nine-year-old quickly abandoned his Legos and ran to the living room to help me. I handed him his one-week-old brother and a half-full bottle and fled to the bathroom.

This became our routine many times a day for several days. A week after we brought home our youngest son, Noah, from the hospital, a violent stomach flu hit our family. The "bug" began with Ian, who was sixteen months old at the time, but like dominoes set up for motion, other family members were soon knocked over from it as well. Four of us suffered from the same grueling symptoms, but thankfully Erik and our newborn escaped the bug.

"I cannot handle this," I kept thinking as I struggled to meet the needs of my family in the midst of complete chaos. I lamented to my husband how disappointed I was with the whole situation. Wasn't having a newborn supposed to be a joyous occasion?

Instead of holding my little one (adopted from birth) and experiencing that special bonding time, I was practically helpless. I was wiped out from the regular duties that come with a new baby (not to mention the work it takes to care for three other children), and I had the added challenge of having to wash and rewash soiled bedding and clean up messes when someone didn't quite make it to the bathroom, all while feeling miserable myself. What threw me completely over the top was the fact that my new pride and joy had severe colic. He cried for five or six hours a day. My husband did what he could to help, but once he started feeling better, he had to return to work. Thank God for Erik.

I called out audibly to God for strength during this difficult time and, I'm sure, whined a bit in the process! But God answers prayers for strength, even whiny ones. I knew from years of walking with Him that sometimes He gives us the physical or emotional strength we need directly. And sometimes He gives strength by providing someone to stand beside us and help. I believe during that overwhelming situation years ago that He provided help through our nine-year-old.

God kept Erik healthy for our family and gave him an enthusiastic willingness to serve. Erik fed and held the baby when my stomach summoned me to the bathroom time and time again. While I tended to another patient in the house, or just needed to lie down and rest, I could count on Erik to be in charge. He didn't demand his way or plead for attention, but he cheerfully did all that I asked. God strengthened my hands and spirit through this little boy.

— Cathy McIlvoy —

My Prayer

Dear Father, life can be quite overwhelming at times.
I thank you that I don't have to go it alone.
You are always with me, and you provide for my needs.
Use me to help give the gift of strength
and encouragement to others in need.
Amen.

31

Liz Cleans House

The greatest among you will be your servant.
~Matthew 23:11

ometimes God's presence alone is not enough, and we need one of his servants to come along and offer support. During my early years of motherhood, I was desperately in need of just that.

With two-year-old Hannah and newborn Sarah, I was suffering from exhaustion. My husband was working the night shift. He slept all morning and part of the afternoon, so I had to try to keep the girls quiet while Daddy slept. He would leave for work at 5:00 p.m. as I was nearing the end of what little energy I had. Then I was left to put the girls to bed and deal with all the nighttime childcare duties alone.

It had been weeks since my house had a decent cleaning. I couldn't remember the last time the kitchen floor had been mopped. Laundry was piling up. Meals were whatever I could scrape together. Living in a fog of sleep deprivation kept me from doing all but the most basic things we needed to get by.

Then a friend listened to the Lord's prompting and picked up the phone.

"How are things going, Marie?" Liz asked.

I thought a moment before responding. Should I say everything's fine, the baby is a delight, and I'm enjoying being a mom? Or should I tell her how things were really going? I opted for the truth.

Ten minutes later, when I was finally done spilling my guts to this friend who had three young children of her own, she asked, "Are you going to be home tomorrow afternoon?"

"Yes. I don't think I'll be going anywhere."

"Good. I'd like to come over and clean your house."

I wasn't sure I heard her right. "You what?" I asked in disbelief.

"I'd like to clean your house. Vacuum, dust, clean the bathroom. When my boys were babies, someone did that for me. It was such a blessing! Now I would like to pass on the blessing to you."

"Well, okay, if you really want to. But what will you do with your kids?"

"My husband has the day off, so they can just stay home with him."

The next day she arrived at the agreed-upon time with a bucket of cleaning supplies in hand and got straight to work. She wouldn't let me lift a finger to help. So I sat and nursed Sarah and read to Hannah while Liz cleaned house. She scrubbed the bathtub till it sparkled. She vacuumed. She dusted. She even mopped the kitchen floor—and all with a smile on her face! The smell of lemon-scented cleaner filled the air. My house hadn't been this clean in months. This was better than any baby shower gift I had received.

I was amazed not just at the cleanliness of my home, but at the effort that this fellow mother put out—for me! In another week, the house was in need of cleaning again. But the memory of Liz cheerfully scrubbing our soap-scum-encrusted bathtub spurred me on to make a better attempt at keeping the house in order.

Now when a friend has a new baby, I wonder how God would like to use me to serve my friend. Cleaning house? Bringing over a meal? Babysitting the older kids so Mom can have a break? Whatever the gift, I know I'll be passing on the blessing of being a servant—the lesson I learned from Liz.

— Marie Cleveland —

My Prayer

Thank you, Lord,
for friends who listen to your voice
and bless us with the gift of their time.
May you always help me keep my eyes
and ears open to ways in which I can be
a blessing to others — even in the midst
of my own busy life.
Amen.

32

Anna Mary's Advice

And let us consider how we may spur
one another on toward love and good deeds.
Let us not give up meeting together,
as some are in the habit of doing,
but let us encourage one another — and
all the more as you see the Day approaching.
~Hebrews 10:24-25

Surprise tinged with a hint of alarm showed on my face at the doctor's words: "You're pregnant!" My husband and I had recently relocated, so when Dick and I heard we were having a baby, we felt understandably overwhelmed!

"We don't really know anyone here yet," I fretted in a phone call to my mother-in-law, Anna Mary. "With no family nearby, who will help us with the baby?"

"You will do just fine," Anna Mary assured me. After a pause, she asked, "Do you remember Harry Sagar, the Methodist pastor?"

"Yes. Nice, quiet guy, right?" I recalled the minister who seemed to exude a calming strength.

"Yes! Harry was so helpful when our church didn't have a pastor, and our family went through a rough patch," she shared. "Did you know he moved to a church near where you and Dick are living?"

"No, I hadn't heard that," I answered, my curiosity piqued.

"You've always been involved in the church. Maybe you could give Harry's church a try. I can find the name of it if you want," she offered.

Her simple, God-inspired suggestion turned out to be the best parenting advice Dick and I ever received. The church was just a mile from our apartment. Though only passing acquaintances with Pastor Sagar, it was nice to see a familiar face when we entered the sanctuary.

Harry introduced us around, and we bonded immediately with the warm, welcoming congregation. One family in particular, the Armels, gathered Dick and me under their wing and treated us like family. In the ensuing months, Lucy, the mother, often invited us to their home.

When I experienced some discomfort close to my due date, we drove to the Armel home to check things out with Lucy. About two hours later, she said, "Pam, I've been watching your face and my watch. You're in labor. I think it's time you headed for the hospital."

Our son was born seven hours later!

Over the years and moves that followed, Anna Mary's advice repeatedly proved to be a blessing from God. Fostered by the wonderful people in the congregation, our children never lacked a grandmotherly hug or a doting babysitter. Like a surrogate family, experienced parents and caring fellow believers became a sounding board for our many questions and gave us the opportunity for some adult conversation.

However, the greatest benefit of involving ourselves in the church was the opportunity to grow spiritually—to cultivate a relationship with God, who then equipped Dick and me to be better partners and parents.

Our children now have kids of their own. They, too, live far from family. Knowing firsthand the parenting challenges they face, I have shared with them the wise counsel that Anna Mary gave me: Find a welcoming church and get involved! There God will provide all the support and encouragement you will ever need.

— Pam Williams —

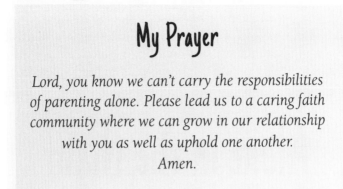

My Prayer

*Lord, you know we can't carry the responsibilities
of parenting alone. Please lead us to a caring faith
community where we can grow in our relationship
with you as well as uphold one another.
Amen.*

33

Alone in the Night

Come to me, all you who are weary and
burdened, and I will give you rest.
~Matthew 11:28

The first six months with our baby twins was such a sleepless blur that I barely remember those precious days. During this time, my husband had an office job, and so he had to get up early in the mornings. Therefore, the lion's share of night duty usually fell to me (although he helped out as much as he could). I often jumped up in the middle of the night at the first sound of crying so that my husband could get enough sleep to enable him to function in the workplace. Saturdays were my only mornings to sleep a little bit as my husband then took over "morning duty." On Sundays, we were both up early again to get everyone ready for church.

I learned very quickly that lack of sleep is often the number-one trial experienced by parents, especially in the first year. New mothers are often advised to "rest when the baby rests," but my two little boys were never sleeping at the same time! But looking back on my many sleepless nights with my babies, it's not the lack of sleep or extreme fatigue that I focus on most. It's the private time that I had with them in the middle of the night when the rest of the household was unconscious.

I remember nursing my babies while rocking back and forth in a chair with the light of the moon shining through the windows. I'd admire their translucent skin, the curve of their little noses, and the perfection of their delicate fingers and toes. Knowing that I had the power to calm their crying and soothe their woes gave me a warm feeling. I'd marvel at each tiny bundle of joy as I held him in my arms.

Whenever I grew too frustrated at not getting enough sleep—and, believe me, it happened quite often—I'd use that time to say my prayers. As I rocked a child to sleep, I'd thank God for the privilege of being that baby's mother. As I coped with a crying infant, I'd remind myself that he was just making his needs known. By focusing on the moment, I could deal with the job at hand, and not tally the hours of sleep I was missing in my head. I also asked God to give my husband and me patience with each other when fatigue shortened our tempers and made us forget we were on this parenting journey together.

Somehow, we survived those sleepless years of babyhood. I realize now it's because I was never alone in the night. I had God's company every step of the way.

— Susan M. Heim —

My Prayer

Dear Father, please allow me to rest in your arms
when I'm feeling weary. Knowing I have you to lean
on when fatigue overwhelms me makes the long,
sleepless nights shorter and sweeter.
Amen.

34

Pregnancy Paranoia

"... The LORD does not look at the things man looks at. Man looks at the outward appearance, but the LORD looks at the heart."
~1 Samuel 16:7

I took a deep breath as the pain from a contraction racked my body. The doors to the hospital waiting room swung open, and a young woman, obviously nine months pregnant, practically bounced through the door carrying a pillow, an overstuffed bag and, of all things, a large exercise ball. Her husband followed, carrying a couple of bags as well. I looked at my own swollen belly and felt like an inferior cream puff. I started to push up out of my chair to meet my husband on his way from the hospital parking garage. Another stabbing contraction pulsed through my lower body, and I sat down hard.

I chastised myself. Why didn't I offer to carry my bag when my husband dropped me off while he parked? Why couldn't I "walk off" my contractions like the other pregnant woman obviously was? And what was the deal with that exercise ball? Was it some new birthing procedure I had failed to research before I went into labor? What kind of mom was I, anyway?

My husband arrived shortly afterward and, on his arm, I hobbled to the maternity ward, stopping every four or five minutes to breathe and deal with the pain of a new contraction. At the check-in counter we saw the bouncy pregnant woman and another dewy-faced, big-bellied woman looking ready to deliver. To my amazement, she was all smiles and calmness. I thought I had entered a maternity ward in *The Twilight Zone*, where moms in labor beamed sweetly instead of screaming in pain. I continued to feel more inferior by the minute. It wasn't until a nurse told me that all inductions were admitted at 6:00 on Monday mornings that I figured out the bizarre behavior of the serene moms.

"They're being induced!" I said loudly, understanding dawning on me. "No wonder they don't look like they are in any pain. I just thought I was a wimp."

"They haven't had the first contraction." The nurse smiled as she placed my IV bag in place.

Later, when I held my peacefully slumbering daughter Gracie in my arms, I felt sheepish about playing the comparison game before she was even born. I may not know about the latest "birthing ball" techniques, but I love Gracie and her older brother Andrew, and am a good mother to them.

It is so easy to look at outward appearances without knowing all the facts. Only God knows all the strengths and weaknesses of individuals, and He has designed each mother's heart to meet the needs of the children with whom she has been blessed. We can be pretty hard on ourselves when we look outward. Thank goodness God looks at the woman within.

— Janeen Lewis —

My Prayer

Dear God, thank you for creating a heart of love inside me for my children. Instead of comparing myself to others, I will look to you for the strength to be the mother I need to be.
Amen.

35

In Death's Shadow

Even though I walk through the valley
of the shadow of death, I will fear no evil,
for you are with me; your rod
and your staff, they comfort me.
~Psalm 23:4

The twenty-third psalm has always been a source of strength for me. Now, looking at the tired, drawn face of my daughter, I needed that strength for her. She was exhausted from almost thirty hours of labor. She never cried out as the pain racked her body, but the pain showed in her eyes as she gripped my hand on one side of her and her husband's on the other.

"Why don't you do something?" I asked the doctor. "She can't take much more."

"You're right," he replied with a look of concern. "Something must have happened to the spinal block. She shouldn't be experiencing this much pain. I'll have to take it out and insert another one. We don't want the baby going into fetal distress."

I watched as the doctor prepared to insert more medication. My daughter looked so helpless, bent over in an almost fetal position. Tears filled my eyes as I thought of the pain and fear she was experiencing. Sensing my emotions, she turned her head slightly and flashed a weak smile.

When you give birth to a child, you watch over her and protect her as she grows, and you never stop trying to make the hurt better, even when she's all grown up. But I couldn't make this better; only God could. I prayed for strength and protection, holding fast to my faith.

As they laid her back on the bed, my daughter closed her eyes in exhaustion. Suddenly, the shrill sound of the monitors exploded in the small room.

"We're losing them. Flip her!" one of the nurses shouted over the noise. Another nurse pushed me toward the door, and I struggled to get around her.

"What's happening?" I cried.

"You have to leave the room so we can take care of your daughter," the nurse replied.

Standing in the corridor outside the door, I kept remembering those chilling words, "We're losing them."

My daughter had prayed many years for a baby. She had miscarried eight years before and was several months into her pregnancy before she let go of the fear of losing this child. Now, on the verge of birth, she faced the specter of death.

It seemed like hours before the doctor called us in to explain what had happened. "Your daughter has a strong, healthy baby, but she has been in labor too long. We have to get the baby out right away. This will require performing a C-section. Her obstetrician is on his way and should be here by the time we have everything ready in surgery."

As they wheeled her to surgery, I felt so helpless, left behind and not knowing what was happening. I called out to God in prayer and continued to pray for strength and protection for my daughter and her baby as time passed.

When my son-in-law walked from the operating room, grinning from ear to ear, my first question was, "How is Bren?"

"She's fine," he replied. Then I looked at the tiny bundle in his arms. Eyes bright and shiny, the baby looked straight into my heart.

I felt so much love fill me.

My daughter's face was tired yet serene when they wheeled her from surgery to the recovery room. She had passed through death's shadow and into the light. They named the baby James, like the apostle. I considered that a fitting name, for he had been born out of our faith in God.

— Brendalyn Crudup —

My Prayer

Father, I thank you for your blessing of life.
I thank you for your strength and guidance.
I pray that you will always hold my child safely
and securely anchored in the palm of your hand.
Amen.

36

Comfort from a Friend

And my God will meet all your needs according to his glorious riches in Christ Jesus.
~Philippians 4:19

One of my greatest blessings started with my son's sniffles, which he "shared" with my husband and me. When nursing my eight-week-old daughter, Lindsey, I coughed and sneezed into my arm in an effort to protect her from illness. I thought my baby had somehow escaped our terrible colds.

A few days later, Lindsey started sleeping more than usual. I attributed it to a growth spurt—until the night she wouldn't sleep for more than thirty minutes at a time. We swayed in the rocking chair and danced around the room, and both of us cried from exhaustion. She developed a strange cough. Something wasn't right.

In the morning, I took her to see the doctor. "Lindsey's working too hard to breathe," our pediatrician said. "I'll call the pediatric floor. Take her straight to the hospital," she urged, with a worried look on her face. "There are a few things we need to rule out." My heart dropped.

I prayed in the car for her safety, but could only imagine the worst.

At the hospital, Lindsey endured a battery of tests and X-rays until it was finally determined she had contracted respiratory syncytial virus (RSV), which can be life-threatening in severe cases. I was terrified.

Our pediatrician called to explain the treatment plan and suggested I go home to rest. "You won't be able to take care of her if you don't get better," she said. Lindsey was connected to oxygen and received frequent breathing treatments. Soon, she could breathe well enough to sleep peacefully. Reluctantly, I decided to head home for a quick nap before my husband got off work and we could return to the hospital together.

I fought back tears in the elevator, guilt-stricken about the severity of Lindsey's illness. Why hadn't I realized how sick she was? How long would she need to be hospitalized? I had let my baby down, and to me, that was unforgivable.

The elevator door opened, and I stepped out into the lobby, nearly bumping into Cynthia, a sweet, caring woman from church. Many young mothers, myself included, looked to her as a role model.

"Hi, Melissa," she said brightly. Then she looked closer at my tear-filled eyes. She pulled me into her arms where, between sobs, I recounted my heartache and fear for Lindsey's life.

"Lindsey's in the hospital now where she'll be able to get well. The doctor and nurses will take good care of her," she assured me. "We'll all pray for her, and she'll be fine."

Cynthia's presence calmed me. She spoke words of comfort and reminded me that God was in control of this situation. Finally regaining composure, I asked Cynthia why she was at the hospital.

"My mother-in-law is here. She's not going to make it much longer," Cynthia explained. I was stunned. Not only had Cynthia put aside her own grief to console and encourage me, but she was there at the hospital at the precise moment I was falling apart. It wasn't a coincidence; God had aligned our paths and knew what I needed to hear. More than ever, I felt God's unfailing love and power. I left the hospital strengthened and hopeful, and was able to rest without worrying. Lindsey spent just two nights in the hospital, and within two weeks made a full recovery, thanks to many prayers.

I reflect often on my "chance" meeting with Cynthia. I'm still amazed that God sent me my own personal comforter in a time of uncertainty. I hope He will use me someday in the same way so others can experience this blessing.

— Melissa Zifzal —

My Prayer

Dear Lord, you always know what we need and when we need it. Thank you for being present in our daily lives and continually proving that your ways and timing are perfect.
Amen.

37

Beating the Bed Rest Blues

A woman giving birth to a child has pain because her time has come; but when her baby is born she forgets the anguish because of her joy that a child is born into the world.
~John 16:21

It was time for my first ultrasound, and I nervously awaited the results. My OB/GYN pulled up the monitor, and I searched the screen for any recognizable picture. There on the screen was a little beating heart. I was overjoyed. As he moved the wand over my rather pregnant belly, he found just what he was looking for: a second heartbeat. It was the first confirmation that my husband and I were to have twins. Not one little bundle to care for, but two. Was I nervous? Was I excited? Was I surprised? Of course, I was all of these and more.

The pregnancy continued, and I experienced the common multiple pregnancy problem of terrible morning sickness. Around the 17th week, I had my first scare when I started bleeding. The doctors put me in the hospital to monitor the situation. I remember praying to God to protect these two beautiful souls inside my body. I waited out the night and, fortunately, the bleeding stopped. They released me the next day, but fear had taken a place in my heart.

It seemed like most of my doctor's visits were checkups to see if anything was wrong. Looking back on them now, I see that I was in such a fearful place. Did I feel an early contraction? Were the babies growing at the correct rate? All these questions and more percolated in my mind.

Being on bed rest in any multiple pregnancy is almost a given, and I was no exception. When the doctor put me on partial bed rest around week 28, I thought he was kidding. I had a two-year-old to care for. My husband was traveling quite a bit. Who was going to care for my daughter, Kara? I tried to stay off my feet, but I was feeling invincible. Staying on the couch for four to six hours a day while caring for a young toddler was not feasible. So I did too much, and I paid for it later.

When I was admitted to the hospital for full bed rest, it finally hit me. I had to slow down and protect these precious bundles inside me. My only job at that point was to keep them inside until week 35 or later. Lying there for two weeks really humbled me. For once in my life, I was dependent on the help of others. I couldn't do it alone anymore. And the amazing thing I realized was that God never expected me to go at it alone. He had back-up help just waiting in the wings all along.

Women from our church sprang into action immediately when my husband announced my hospitalization at prayer time during the service. They signed up to bring meals to the house and even arranged babysitting for my daughter. I received visitors in the hospital, and one lovely person painstakingly tried to show me how to needlepoint. No longer was I fearful. I felt hope because I had God's loving arms wrapped around me.

Reflecting back on it now, God was there each and every step of the way. He had a plan for me to be a mother of twins, and my womb was a place for these dear babies to grow. They needed me just as much as I so desperately needed Him.

In hindsight, I wish that I had given my worries to God much earlier. But, with God's help and the gift of friendship from others, I made it to 36½ weeks before delivering. Our twins were born healthy and ready to take on the world—and our life.

— Karen C. Talcott —

My Prayer

Dear Lord, thank you for the loving care that you always provide for me. I feel so blessed that I am part of a church family that steps into action when someone is in need.
Amen.

38

God, Give Me Strength

*But those who hope in the LORD will renew
their strength. They will soar on wings like eagles;
they will run and not grow weary,
they will walk and not be faint.*
~Isaiah 40:31

I held my screaming infant, purposefully stroked his cheek, kissed his forehead, whispered "I love you," carefully swaddled him in a cozy baby blue blanket, and placed him gently in his crib. Moments later, I sat on the shower floor, knees drawn up to my chest, water pummeling my back. And I wept.

Motherhood has been the most rewarding, delightful experience of my life. It has brought me joy and exhilaration, and an overwhelming sense of love that I never knew existed. But motherhood has also brought some of my life's most trying and tiring experiences.

When I was twelve, I was diagnosed with narcolepsy, a sleep disorder caused by the brain's inability to regulate sleep-wake cycles. With this condition, I often feel overwhelming daytime sleepiness. Over time, I've learned that by taking naps, exercising, and going to bed early, I'm able to control the severity of the sleepiness. But as I adjusted to new motherhood, I found it difficult, as most new mothers do, to make time to exercise, take a nap, or go to bed early. I was unable to do what I needed to control the symptoms. Now I found myself in a moment of excruciating exhaustion.

My patience had run out, as well as the methods I normally used to console my infant. I rocked and fed him, changed his diaper, and even took him for a walk outside. I tried the pacifier, toys, and soothing music. Nothing worked, and I felt completely broken.

Steam from the warm water enveloped me, and I bent my head in prayer, asking God to restore my spirit. As God's peace flowed through me and the cleansing water washed away my tears, I eventually regained my composure. After getting dressed, I walked back to my baby's room and cautiously opened the door. Peering into the crib, I saw that he had finally drifted off to dreamland. With my son safe and sound in his room, I went back to my room and fell into a deep, restorative sleep. I awoke two hours later, completely renewed, as the baby monitor relayed the precious sounds of his coos and giggles. God showed His presence in that moment by giving me the strength to face parenting anew.

— Michelle Sedas —

My Prayer

Dear God, please give me strength to endure the trying moments of motherhood. When I feel that I'm barely hanging on, let your peace fill my heart. Allow my house to be a place of refuge, filled with your tranquility and serenity.
Amen.

39

That Kind of Faith

*When Jesus heard this, he was amazed at him,
and turning to the crowd following him,
he said, "I tell you, I have not found
such great faith even in Israel."*
~Luke 7:9

The backyard is a great place for adventure. And if there is an adventure to be found, my son, Colin, will find it. This week, he was in full Jedi costume (Obi-Wan Kenobi hooded cape, matching brown pants that happen to belong to a Peter Pan costume, long-sleeved white T-shirt, black boots, light saber—just so you have a visual). As I was cooking dinner, he blasted through the back door, red-faced and happy.

"Mama, this is so cool. You want to know what I did?"

In this moment, I paused because I wasn't actually sure I wanted to know what he did, even though I may have needed to know. After a few seconds of debate in my head, I cautiously asked, "What?"

Colin proceeded to tell me that he took one of the scrap 2x4s in the backyard and stretched it from the Little Tikes fort to the Little Tikes playhouse. Then, with great skill and dexterity, he crawled across the precariously placed scrap of wood from the fort to the top of the playhouse. The top of the playhouse is not flat, so the wood could have easily slid right off the plastic roof and onto the ground—with one six-year-old Jedi riding along.

"Colin, that was not safe! You should not have done that. You could have gotten hurt."

"No, Mama. When I crawled across it, I just said, 'God is with me, God is with me,' until I got to the other side."

My son believed wholeheartedly that if God was with him, nothing bad could happen. I quickly told him that God was with him, but He also gave him a brain to think with, and that brain should have told him that crawling on the board wasn't a good idea.

Later, I got to thinking about what Colin had said. "God is with me." Colin had complete faith in God. That is some kind of faith. That is the kind of faith with which I would like to face each day. I'm not going to do any tightrope walking between the neighbor's house and mine, but I would like to walk with the confidence of a six-year-old Jedi, wise beyond his years. Wouldn't you?

— Carol Hatcher —

My Prayer

Lord, help me to come to you with the faith of a child. Let me always remember the sweet and simple words, "God is with me." With you, nothing is impossible.
Amen.

40

Listen to the Children

The wolf will live with the lamb, the leopard will lie down with the goat, the calf and the lion and the yearling together; and a little child will lead them.
~Isaiah 11:6

My husband and I have a blended family of nine grandchildren, and these days I thrill when one of them summons, "Nana!" One day, our verbose little Madison, then four, yanked me—not by the hand, but by my heartstrings—so hard it brought me to my knees.

After a particularly hectic day of teaching preschoolers, I drove home anxious to kick off my shoes and relax on the couch for fifteen minutes to enjoy the silence. I was surprised when Madison threw open the front door and greeted me.

"I've been here with Grandpa all day," she screeched. "I've been waiting for YOU, Nana!"

I was delighted to see her, but I needed a break from non-stop chatter. Before I could set down my purse, she noticed my gold filigree locket—a miniature coin purse with a clasp that opened. I scooped her up and gave her a hug. She tugged at the chain and started with a barrage of unstoppable questions.

"Nana, where did you get that little purse necklace? What's inside that little purse necklace? Do you have candy or pennies inside your little purse necklace? Does that little purse necklace open? I see there's a closer on it. Let me look in there."

"Nothing is in there, honey; it's empty," I said, with a twinge of irritation in my voice.

She followed me from room to room as I unloaded my belongings. "I know a penny would fit in there, or maybe one M&M. There has to be something in there. I just know there's something in that little purse necklace. Open it!" she demanded.

I plopped down on the sofa. She climbed in my lap and fiddled with the pendant.

"There IS something in here," she insisted as she tried to unclasp it.

"No, there is not," I countered impatiently.

"There is, too." She turned my head and looked into my eyes. "I know it for sure." Her strawberry-blond curls bobbed up and down. Her blue eyes danced with pleasure, and she grinned from ear to ear. "Open it, and you'll see what's in there, Nana," she said confidently as she shoved the little coin purse under my nose.

"It is empty. See!" I yanked open the clasp.

"No, it's not. Look! Nana, I told you something was inside. See? It's filled with God's love. God's love is everywhere, even in your little gold purse necklace," she shouted exuberantly.

Her comment knocked the wind out of me. Too often we go about our busy days hearing our children prattle, but not really taking the time to listen. As the Bible tells us in Isaiah 11:6, "... a little child will lead..."

— Linda O'Connell —

My Prayer

Lord, as I go through my busy day,
help me to slow down, bend down to a child's level,
and remember to bow down to you.
Help me to use gentle words and a kind voice.
Open my heart and ears so that I may hear your
message in the words of children.
Amen.

41

She Needed a Hug

*He who loves a pure heart and whose speech
is gracious will have the king for his friend.*
~Proverbs 22:11

When a teacher calls you over to talk about your son, it's not surprising that a wave of "oh, no" comes over you—especially when your son is the kind of person who loves to make people laugh, even in class. My son is one of those people. If he notices heaviness in the room, he will do just about anything to lighten the mood. We had been working with him to understand that there are appropriate times and places to do this, but sometimes he still struggled with it. So when his teacher called me over after a field trip one day, I got that sinking feeling.

Every Christmas season, our Christian school takes different classes of kids to sing at the nursing homes in our area. This year, my son Jesse's class was going to visit with the residents. A smaller group was going to see the Alzheimer's patients. Jesse had been hand-selected to go into this locked unit.

When the teacher called me over to discuss Jesse's actions after the nursing home visit, I simply didn't know what to think. My father-in-law, who had dementia, lived with us for a while, and I knew that

Jesse understood what these people were going through, and how upset they could get if there was a commotion. But I also knew that he might try to help his friends feel happier if they were getting uncomfortable at the nursing home.

The teacher told me that as the children were passing one door, they noticed a little lady sitting on her bed, watching them pass. Jesse saw her and, without asking, went into her room and gave her a hug. She started to softly cry, as did the teacher and several of the students. Seeing their tears, my tenderhearted son came out looking like a whipped puppy and asking if he did something wrong.

The teacher simply asked, "What made you go in there?"

"She looked like she needed a hug," he responded. "I'm sorry. I didn't mean to make her cry."

Thankfully, the teacher wrapped her arms around Jesse and told him the truth.

"Jesse, your arms were the arms of Jesus today. She obviously needed that hug. Thank you for loving her the way He loves her."

— Lorie Bibbee —

My Prayer

Dear Heavenly Father, thank you for loving us through the arms of others. Teach us to love you in spirit and truth, and help me to never correct the tenderheartedness out of my child.
Amen.

42

Beautiful Things

*"You are the light of the world. A city on a hill
cannot be hidden. Neither do people light a lamp and
put it under a bowl. Instead they put it on its stand,
and it gives light to everyone in the house.
In the same way, let your light shine before men,
that they may see your good deeds and
praise your Father in heaven."*
~Matthew 5:14-16

When my daughter Kayla was four, she came into my room to watch me dress. She found a pair of heels I'd only worn once or twice because they pinched my feet.

"Mommy, wear these."

"I don't like them."

"But they're so beautiful."

Somehow, I convinced her that my tennis shoes were fine. She rummaged through my jewelry box, bringing necklaces, bracelets, and earrings I never wear.

"Put these on, Mommy."

"I don't want to."

"But they're so beautiful."

I convinced her to drop the idea of jewelry. She went back into my closet, dragging out a long-forgotten evening gown.

"You should wear this today."

"It's too small."

"But it's so beautiful."

We argued over more items — make-up, accessories, even my underwear. She couldn't understand why I had so many beautiful things I never wore. Most of them had been purchased for special occasions but were never comfortable.

She finally accepted my wardrobe of jeans, sweatshirt, no make-up, and hair in a ponytail. I selected a pair of jeans for her.

"Mommy, I don't like these."

"But they're easy to play in."

"They're not comfortable. I want to wear this." She pointed to a Christmas dress in the back of the closet.

"You can't wear a Christmas dress in the spring."

"I don't care. It's pretty and sparkly, and I want to wear it."

I looked through her closet for shoes. I found some black Mary Janes. They were practical and matched the dress nicely.

"You picked the wrong shoes."

"But they match your dress."

"No, they don't. They're not sparkly like my dress. I want to wear my sparkle shoes."

She then rummaged through her toys, pulling out bracelets, necklaces, and every other item she considered jewelry and piled it on. She stuck a variety of ribbons and bows of every color in her hair. "I'm making myself beautiful."

Her statement bothered me. I never want her to think that things are what make us beautiful. I tried explaining this principle to her, wanting to instill the value of true beauty in her. With innocent blue eyes, she looked at me.

"Of course, I'm beautiful. That's why I wear beautiful things. You're beautiful, too. That's why you should wear your beautiful things instead of hiding them in the closet."

How many times do we hide the beautiful things in our lives, saving them for that perfect moment? We do this not only in the realm of fashion, but even in the wonderful qualities we have inside us. By the time we get around to using our beautiful things, they no longer fit or have lost their shine. Their beauty has been wasted. Not my daughter. She uses every beautiful thing for the purpose for which it was created.

— Danica Favorite —

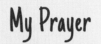

My Prayer

Lord, help me to enjoy every beautiful thing you give us and not let it go to waste.
What a truly wonderful world you have created! I am so fortunate to be a witness to your beautiful gifts each and every day.
Amen.

43

Resting in Hope

*Therefore my heart is glad and my tongue rejoices;
my body also will rest secure.*
~Psalm 16:9

Sometimes, life is just difficult. As a mother, it is frustrating when our children say mean things to each other and fight over toys. It is difficult when the clothes dryer quits and the dog gets sick. And how many times has a day gone by and you realized you forgot to take a shower? Hope helps.

One day, my ten-year-old son Noah and I were driving down a heavily trafficked street when my car started dying and then completely stopped. After a couple of minutes, it started again, only to die once more a block up the street. I pointed the car toward the repair shop, but we stopped and started several times along the way.

Hope leaked out of me like the transmission fluid leaked out of my car. Frustration crept in. By our third stop and start, I was angry.

In tears, I asked, "Noah, will you pray for me?"

My son prayed, "God, please help Mom not be so frustrated and help us make it to the mechanic's. And help Mom know that this is a tiny little problem compared to the rest of the world."

Truth and perspective. My little man was full of hope. When the hopeful help the hopeless, I think God applauds. Giving hope is a beautiful transaction, born of love and selflessness. It is especially lovely when a child gives hope to a parent.

We made it to the auto shop where my car was pronounced dead. Transmission problems. That's like terminal cancer for cars.

At home, my husband and I talked about our situation. Hope must be consciously invited into a discussion of finances when money is tight. It is so easy to give up and dwell on thoughts like, "Can't we ever get ahead?" and "Why do we always end up dipping into savings?" After a tense discussion, John and I prayed and made some decisions. Hope arrived with a plan in his hand.

That night, I hugged my son tightly and thanked him for his prayer in the car. God used my son's words to whack me in the head. Noah was right. The death of a car is not reason to lose hope and despair. Why? Because we have the hope of Christ. We've made a decision in faith to lean on the supernatural, invisible God who allows joy and doesn't always shield pain.

We hope.

If you are discouraged by this economy or by loneliness or by the endless exhaustion of being a mother, I urge you to look up and lie back. Rest in His hope, and He will carry you through. Even when life is difficult.

— Robbie Iobst —

My Prayer

*God, thank you for the knowledge
that you are in control and will carry us through.
Remind me to rest in that hope
and then teach it to my children.
And help me to listen when
my children are the carriers of your divine message.
Amen.*

44

A Daughter's Eyes

*"And why do you worry about clothes? See how the
lilies of the field grow. They do not labor or spin."*
~Matthew 6:28

"Cate, please get the groceries for me. I'm a mess and don't
want to go in."

As a single parent, farming isn't always a great occupation.
If a woman has to make an appearance in the nearest town,
having some time to scrub up a bit helps. But that day, my timing was
off, and I still had more repairing to do on the seeder before the next
day's planting. There was just enough daylight left to get the kids, run
to the store, and hurry back for another round with the beast.

During my childhood, my dad always scrubbed up, changed
clothes, and put on his wedding ring before going to town from the
ranch. Though I had once been a fashion designer, choosing models and
toasting champagne, I now followed in my father's chosen occupation.
But unlike my father, I had no spouse to run small errands or time to
scrub up on a weekday run to town. So with fingernails blackened
by grease and a smudge on my cheek (missed in a quick clean-up), I
dashed to pick up the kids and grab some necessities.

Now I sat embarrassed by my unladylike appearance, asking my teenage daughter to go into the store for me. But Cate kept insisting that I come. Getting a bit frustrated, I explained that I was just too dirty to be seen in public. Her response shocked me and moved my exhausted heart.

"Mom, I'm proud of your hands. They show that you're not afraid to do anything. I don't know any other mom who works so hard. I want you to come in with us."

In my daughter's eyes, I was beautiful and someone to be proud of, even smudged with grease and burnt by the sun. Of course, I joined her, still embarrassed, but feeling very loved.

— Cecilia McNeal —

My Prayer

Lord, thank you for this day
in which the "fruit of my womb,"
your ultimate gift to me,
can teach me about true beauty.
Open my eyes and heart to the simplicity
and beauty of a child's love.
Amen.

45

The Nativity Lesson

My eyes are ever on the LORD,
for only he will release my feet from the snare.
~Psalm 25:15

It was a gorgeous autumn day, but I was oblivious to the golden leaves fluttering along my drive home from a day of teaching first graders. My mind still lingered in the classroom, wondering how I would get assessments done by the following week and wishing I could find the right approach for a little boy struggling with addition. Soon, my mind raced forward to my family at home. My four-year-old daughter and husband would be hungry. What leftovers did we have in the refrigerator? My stressed-out mind seemed to be a symptom of the life I led as a teacher and mother.

That evening as I watched my daughter put on a puppet show, my eyes struggled to stay open, and I kept thinking about the clean laundry that needed folding. Each day, I leaned on God for strength, but under constant demands and endless work, I often found the day stripped of all peace and joy. I longed to feel God's peaceful presence in every moment, but my harried circumstances didn't match the peace and joy God promised to give.

One Sunday afternoon in December, my daughter, Leah, and I

got out our nativity sets. I spent a few extra minutes placing the ceramic figures in just the right places, making sure the sheep were just the right distance from the shepherds and that the figures were balanced on each side of Jesus. I looked at Leah. She had her very own set of nativity figures, a gift from friends when she was a year old. Made of hard rubber and bright colors, they were her year-round companions. Mary and Joseph had taken many rides on her circus train. This Christmas, she was placing them on our coffee table in an unusual way. She placed Jesus in the center, and all of the other figures stood around him in a tight circle, staring intently at the baby in the manger.

When I asked Leah about the arrangement, she said simply, "They want to see Jesus."

I stared, awestruck at the illustration before me. Wasn't this God's desire for us? To see Jesus. To place Jesus right at the center of our lives and to keep our eyes on Him. I looked at the figures in my own nativity set and saw each character staring off in many different directions with not so much as a glance toward Jesus. It was just like the life I was trying to lead—focusing my eyes on the circumstances around me, rather than Jesus. From that moment on, I resolved to keep Jesus as the center of my life.

Sharing each moment of the day with my Savior became complete joy. When I had a decision to make, I prayed. When I felt burdened, I released the burden to God. Whatever I lacked, I asked God to provide. Instead of being tossed about by my hectic schedule, I used each circumstance to draw closer to God. I found the peace and joy I longed for. And each year at Christmas, we set the figures in the nativity set around Jesus and let them stare intently on Him because that is God's desire for us... all year long.

— Janice M. Gibson —

My Prayer

Dear God, it is so easy for me to get caught up in the circumstances of this busy life I lead as a mother. Please help me to keep my eyes on you, and to know that you are my source for all things in this life. Amen.

46

A Race Run Well

Do you not know that in a race all the runners run,
but only one gets the prize? Run in such a way
as to get the prize.
~1 Corinthians 9:24

My son, Nick, loves sports: running, hitting balls, shooting baskets, you name it. But what he loves even more is to have his father and me there on the sidelines watching him. So, naturally, for his kindergarten field day, I was there ready and waiting, camera in hand to watch him run the 200-yard dash.

Though it was a sunny May morning, the night before had brought enough rain that the morning sun didn't have time to dry the ground, so it was slick. Seven kindergarten boys were standing at the ready, bodies wiggling in anticipation for the flag to fall. It did, and they ran. Nick pushed his way to the lead and ran for all he was worth. My camera clicked constantly, trying to capture my son's body as it flew past me toward the finish line.

But then he fell, his feet sliding out from under him and across the wet grass. Every mother knows what it feels like when her child falls, whether literally or figuratively. For Nick, that moment in the grass was defining for him. He looked at me bewildered, not sure what to do. Was he going to give up and walk the rest of the way? Would he cry? Would he even finish? I could see the wheels turning furiously in his head.

I started shouting. "Get up! Keep going!" I must have looked ridiculous, shouting and jumping up and down like a maniac with my camera flying around my neck, but it was enough to encourage my son to get up and finish. He did more than finish. He won, propelled by a determination that I had never seen in him up to that point.

I like to think that, as his mom, it was my screaming and jumping that did it. It probably was. After all, he was only six, and I was still cool. But it reminded me at that moment of God, and how He is there to encourage us when we fall, whether it's through a kind word from a friend, through His Word or some other way. God is a God of encouragement. He wants us to succeed. Sometimes, success is just the act of finishing what we've started and not letting the circumstances around us determine how we will behave.

I was so proud of Nick that day—not for winning, but for getting up and doing what needed to be done—the determination, the work, the payoff. May we be willing to do what God has called us to do as moms—to work, be tenacious, and never give up.

— Kathryn Nielson —

My Prayer

Lord, I pray that you will give me
the encouragement to finish the tasks
that you have given me to do in this life.
Please grant me tenacity and the desire
to finish well so that when I see you face-to-face,
I will be able to hear you say, "Well done.
Amen.

47

Twenty-Five-Cent Pearls

A good name is more desirable than great riches;
to be esteemed is better than silver or gold.
~Proverbs 22:1

Many years ago, when my younger son, Chris, was eight years old, he taught me a very poignant lesson about what it means to be wealthy. Our family had just settled into a new home, and my four children—two boys and twin girls—hadn't yet had a chance to make many friends. To them, that first summer in our new surroundings seemed long and just a tad boring. One hot July morning, however, we found that our next-door neighbor, Sandie, was having a garage sale. Excited by this turn of events, my kids hurried over to go "shopping." Three of them soon came home with their treasures, but Chris, who had a whole twenty-five cents to his name, lingered in Sandie's garage. It seemed that Sandie had some costume jewelry for sale, and nestled within her display of used baubles was a strand of pearls that Chris particularly wanted.

"My mom doesn't have much jew-el-er-ry," he proclaimed, stumbling on that last word with bright-eyed charm. "She sure would like a necklace."

"Would she?" asked Sandie, amused.

The problem was that Sandie had priced the pearls at a dollar, but Chris only had that one lone quarter in hand. He was determined, though, my boy, and began bartering with Sandie, offering not only his quarter but to do chores in exchange for the pearls. Touched, Sandie acquiesced.

"Mom! Mom!" Chris called to me when he came running home. "Close your eyes!"

I did as directed, and when he asked me to open my eyes — and my gift — I followed that directive, too. "Oh, sweetheart," I said at last. "These are beautiful."

"Sandie let me wrap them for you and everything. Do you really like them?"

"You know I do."

The pearls lay neatly in my hand, gleaming in the soft summer light, only to be outdone by my son's smile. "Try them on," he insisted.

Again, I did as he requested to the sound of his gasps of delight.

"Those will be the most expensive pearls you'll ever own," Sandie later told me wisely.

I couldn't have agreed with her more.

In our materialistic, get-ahead world, it's sometimes easy to forget what really matters — that love is God's greatest gift. While it has no price tag or overt dollar amount, love is also our greatest wealth, the shimmering pearl in the rough palm of our hand, the very currency by which we connect with each other. As mothers, we are charged with teaching our children this early important lesson. And sometimes, if we're lucky, our children teach the lesson to us. I believe it's more than mere coincidence that, all these years later, a set of pearl earrings was one of the first gifts Chris gave to his bride Nicole. For me, that held a double meaning, and on the night before their wedding, I whispered this fervent prayer: May they always have twenty-five-cent pearls.

— Theresa Sanders —

My Prayer

How quickly we forget, dear God,
what true wealth really means.
Help me to remember to spend my currency well,
and, having taught this to my children as best I knew
how, let me always remain open to the lessons they
teach me. Bless my babies, Father, even when they
are all admirably grown.
They have been—and will always be—
the pearls that grace the rough palm of my hand
Amen.

48

Riding the Rollercoaster

Being confident of this, that he who began a
good work in you will carry it on to completion
until the day of Christ Jesus.
~Philippians 1:6

I used to think I was in control. I'm a mother, after all. And raising two older boys led me to believe I knew what to expect with the youngest. Of course, knowing adolescence was about to take over our home for the third time didn't mean I was thrilled about it.

Not. One. Bit.

As in so many other areas of his life, my youngest entered his teen years with a flare for the dramatic. Smart, handsome, and charming, this gangly preteen held more talent and charisma in his little twelve-year-old finger than most could hope to have in a lifetime. Everywhere we went, friends and strangers commented on what an exceptional young man he was becoming:

"I love your son."

"He's so funny!"

"What a bright child. He probably talks circles around his teachers."

Yes, yes, and yes. He was that and much more.

But it's the "much more" that was giving me a fit.

With all that talent came a volatile combination of both overconfidence and deep insecurity. One moment, he arrogantly pronounced his absolute independence; the next, he crawled up in my lap longing to be loved. I'd stepped onto the adolescent rollercoaster without an end in sight.

After picking him up from a church event one evening, this child who normally couldn't stop talking sat strangely quiet in the back seat of my car. I gave it a couple of minutes, but then my curiosity got the best of me.

"Everything okay?"

"Yeah." A one-word answer. Something was definitely wrong.

"You sure? You haven't said much since you got in the car."

He answered me with silence, and I didn't know whether to press or back off. Within a couple more minutes, he finally spoke, his voice strained.

"You know, Mom, I realized something tonight."

"Really? What's that?"

"In spite of all the things I don't do right, God loves me. I mean, He really does."

Eyes wet with tears and bright with hope, he went on to explain how the truth of God's love — His personal love — hit him like an arrow to the heart. And for that moment, the insecure not-yet-a-man understood something many men through the ages have never fully grasped: God's love is unconditional.

I learned something, too, that night. Although there are moments when I'm unsure of how to parent my boys, when I struggle to control situations or find the words or methods to teach them to be the men I want them to be, someone bigger than me is working in the hearts and lives of my children. And what He started, He will finish.

Until then, I'm merely a white-knuckled momma on the roller-coaster of a lifetime. And loving every minute of it.

Well, almost.

— Michele Cushatt —

My Prayer

*God, I like to think I'm in charge,
but the truth is YOU are. Thank you for leading my
children places I can't take them. And for loving them
unconditionally every step of the way.
Amen.*

49

The Boring, Old Prayer

*...The prayer of a righteous man is powerful
and effective.*
~James 5:16

"Dear God, thank you for keeping us safe today and thank you for this food," my nine-year-old son, Jordan, prayed over his dinner one evening. "Thank you for giving me good parents and for sending Jesus to die on the cross for our sins. You are so good to us, Lord. Please help tomorrow to be a good day, too. In Jesus' name, amen."

"Amen," we all repeated before starting in on our evening meal.

That night at bedtime, when I was tucking Jordan in, he shrugged one shoulder and said, "Mom, I don't want to pray tonight."

"Why? What's wrong?" I asked, concerned.

"Nothing's wrong," he said. "It's just that every time I pray, I say the same things. I can't think of anything new to pray about, and I'm sure God is tired of hearing the same boring, old prayer night after night."

"Oh, Jordan, that's not true. God wants us to pray, no matter what we say. It's all right to say the same things over and over again, as long as we say them," I said.

He shook his head. "I just don't want to tonight, Mom."

"God just wants us to talk to Him, no matter what we say," I insisted, but Jordan was equally insistent that God was tired of hearing his "boring, old prayer."

I sighed and left Jordan's room, concerned that I had failed to get through to my son on this important issue. I immediately took my concerns to the Lord, and He provided me with an answer right away.

I went back into Jordan's room, sat on the edge of his bed, and said, "I love you, Jordan."

He smiled, already sleepy, and said, "I love you, too, Mom."

I repeated the words three more times, and by then, he was fully awake and giggling. "Why do you keep saying that to me?" he asked.

Instead of answering him, I said, "Jordan, thank you for helping with the dishes tonight."

He gave me a funny look and said, "You're welcome."

"Jordan, you are a wonderful son, and I am so glad to be your mom," I said.

He smiled and hugged me, and then said, "Did you come back in here and wake me up just to say nice things to me?"

"Yes, I did. Are you tired of hearing nice things?"

He shook his head. "No, I like it. It makes me feel good."

"Are you bored?"

Again he shook his head. "Nope, I'm not bored. You can keep going if you want to."

I laughed a bit and said, "So you like it when I say nice things to you, right?"

He nodded.

"How do you think it makes God feel when we say nice things to Him?"

"I'm sure He likes it, too." He thought for a minute, finally realizing the point I was making. "You think God likes my boring, old prayer, don't you?"

"Yes, I do. I think it makes God feel good when we thank Him for what He gives us, even if we thank Him for those things every single day. God just wants our praise."

He nodded. "So no prayer is boring to God, right, Mom?"

"That's right. God wants to hear from us, even if we say the same things all the time."

Jordan grabbed my hand and closed his eyes. "Dear God, thank you for my mom. I think I already said that today, but I know you won't mind hearing it again."

— Diane Stark —

My Prayer

Dear Lord, thank you for hearing our prayers,
no matter how small they may seem to us.
Thank you for caring about our problems, sharing
our joys, and always, always being there for us.
Amen.

50

Meltdown in My Heart

*Listen to my cry for help, my King and my God,
for to you I pray. In the morning, O LORD,
you hear my voice; in the morning I lay my requests
before you and wait in expectation.*
~Psalm 5:2-3

The morning started out in a mad dash because I did something I never do: I overslept. For most people, that wouldn't be such a big deal, but my ten-year-old son, Rett, is autistic. Sudden changes in routine frighten him because he cannot process outside stimuli quickly enough to respond. Any disruption in routine frustrates and angers Rett and usually results in a meltdown.

As I helped Rett get dressed, I kept repeating, "Mom overslept, so we need to hurry, okay?"

"Okay," he droned, but didn't move any faster.

For a while, I thought we were making progress. Rett sat with one shoe off and one shoe on when I heard the bus honk. Oh, no, he's going to miss the bus! I ran out and motioned for the driver to please wait a minute. If Rett didn't get to ride the bus to school, he would surely have a meltdown. I scurried back into the house, helped him put on his other shoe, and then rushed him out the door. Too late.

The bus was gone.

"Oh, no!" Rett cried. "It's gone!" His obvious distress confirmed my worst fears. A meltdown was inevitable.

Still, I tried to defuse the situation. "That's okay, bud. Mom will take you this morning." I used my most soothing voice.

Silence. I looked at Rett's disappointed little face and waited, expecting him to jump up and down and flap his arms. I waited for him to emit high-pitched squeals and pace from one end of the room to the other, repeating, "Oh, no. Oh, no…" punctuated by a self-inflicted slap to the head. Yes, I waited — but nothing happened.

After breakfast, Rett hung his head and shuffled out to the car as if his shoulders had suddenly turned into stone. "Lord, please don't let him stay angry with me," I prayed. "And please don't let this destroy his whole day."

That's when I realized we'd missed the most important part of our daily routine — morning prayer. That day, Rett said the prayer I had taught him in the car as traffic whizzed by, and all kinds of sights, sounds, and smells assailed his already overloaded senses.

When we arrived at school, I handed him over to his teacher. "You have a good day now, Rett, okay?" It was more a plea than a request. I felt like I'd held my breath the whole way over just waiting for the inevitable outburst.

"Okay," he said, his voice void of expression.

I started to drive away, my heart heavy with guilt for marring one precious day of Rett's already difficult life. As I eased over the first speed bump, I heard Rett yell, "Hey, Mom!" My window was down, so I could hear him, but I couldn't see him without turning around.

"What, honey?" I tried to sound calm, but inside I cringed. Oh, no. Here comes the meltdown.

Rett couldn't hear me, so he continued to yell, "Hey, Mom. Hey, Mom. HEY, MOM!"

By then I had stopped. I looked over to find Rett running toward the car, dragging his teacher behind him. As soon as he reached the passenger window, we made eye contact. "I love you, Mom," he said. Then he put his little hand to his lips and blew me kisses.

And that's when the meltdown finally came... not in Rett, but right inside my heart.

— Tracie "Sissy" Taylor —

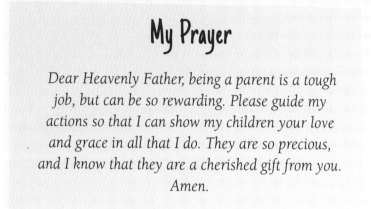

My Prayer

Dear Heavenly Father, being a parent is a tough job, but can be so rewarding. Please guide my actions so that I can show my children your love and grace in all that I do. They are so precious, and I know that they are a cherished gift from you. Amen.

51

Never Alone

"...And surely I am with you always,
to the very end of the age."
~Matthew 28:20

It was the middle of the night. Her fever was steadily climbing, and as a first-time mom, I was scared out of my wits! She was only three and ever so sick. She began to cry and pull at her ear. I checked her temperature once more: 104 degrees. I had already tried tepid baths. Nothing was working. The doctor had told me when I called that if the fever continued to rise, we should go to the nearest emergency room.

My husband was working, and we lived out in the country. I bundled her up and headed for the car. It was snowing, and I had heard on the evening news there was a lot of ice on the roads. They kept telling everyone to stay home. But the hospital was only five miles away, and I knew I had to get there. Could I make it with the snow coming down rapidly and freezing as soon as it hit the road?

As I backed out of the driveway, I said a prayer.

"Dear God, please be with us. Help me get there safely."

I looked back at my baby in her car seat. She was still crying and pulling at her ear. I said another prayer as I pulled onto the highway.

I could feel the tires slipping.

In the car, I sensed we were not alone. I remembered the words to a song I had sung many years ago in church called "Never Alone." God's promises never to leave us rang within my soul.

We made it to the hospital, and my daughter was diagnosed with a double ear infection. Her fever went down.

Later, as we started toward home, I looked at her. The crying was over, and she was sleeping ever so peacefully. I smiled.

That night, on an icy road with a sick child, I had another passenger in the car and a companion in the hospital. God sat beside me, guiding me and reassuring me of those words I had sung so long ago. We are "Never Alone."

— Marsha B. Smith —

My Prayer

*Dear Lord, thank you so much
for your divine presence, which is always with us.
When we feel alone, we have only to remember
your promise and your presence surrounds us.
Thank you, God, for staying by our sides during all
the crises in our lives.
Amen.*

52

Abandoned? Not Ever!

...God has said, "Never will I leave you; never will I forsake you."
~Hebrews 13:5

Cancer patients, chemotherapy, and side effects were my child's companions after she was diagnosed with leukemia at age eleven. Those were frightening times for Karin, as well as for me. As she lay stark white in a cold hospital bed, her little hand grabbed mine, and she said, "Mommy, don't leave me."

In my heart, I was determined not to let her down. I couldn't bear to leave Karin's bedside. When I had to leave the hospital, I made sure another family member was there to replace me.

Some of the little children we met in the hospital were not so fortunate. One little boy, blinded by a brain tumor, had been deserted by his family. The hospital and the staff were now his adopted home and family.

I sobbed over the injustice of this child's dilemma. How could his family abandon him in his hour of need? Evidently, the burden of meeting his health and financial requirements were beyond the scope of what they could contend with. He was discarded like a worn-out shoe.

I have to admit that I was feeling just as abandoned. I cried out to God and asked, "Why? Why are all these things happening to my child? How will we overcome all the obstacles? Are you up there listening, God?"

I felt His answer come to me, not in an audible voice, but in the love showered on me and my family by those He sent to help us: a macaroni and cheese dish delivered to the hospital for Karin, a crocheting project for me to work on in the hospital, an unexpected visit from a stranger, money donated by another stranger, a weekend trip to the shore on a break from chemo… all these things and more told of the loving watchfulness of my Heavenly Father.

Things don't always work out according to our plans. None of us is immune to the heartaches and difficulties of life, but through all our trials I have learned to rely on God's promise: "Never will I leave you; never will I forsake you" (Hebrews 13:5).

— Pat Moyer —

My Prayer

Thank you, Heavenly Father, for providing the help I need to make it through some of the toughest times a parent can know. Thank you for showing me that you are always there to help me.
I know that I am not abandoned.
Amen.

53

The Grab Bag

*Now faith is being sure of what we hope for
and certain of what we do not see.*
~Hebrews 11:1

"**M**ommy, why do we pray?"

The sweet timbre of my four-year-old daughter's voice stopped me short as I buckled her into the car seat at the start of our journey to the grocery store. A religious question normally would have been a no-brainer for me. Raised Protestant, I was certain I could answer anything a preschooler threw at me. But, for several months, I'd been drifting through a period of self-reflection about my own spiritual convictions. Those periods of doubt would pop up every so often, but they always left me with renewed faith.

With her face inches from mine, her innocent blue eyes stared back, waiting for an answer. No need to dwell on my lingering concerns, I thought before I spoke. She's too young for me to answer with editorial comments anyway.

"Praying is a way to speak to God."

"Could I ask for things?" she prodded.

At least it wasn't a question about where babies come from.

"Well, we pray if we need help or when we're sad or want something special to happen."

I shut her car door and got into the driver's seat. "What would you ask God for, honey?"

"A Slinky."

Her answer surprised me, but it wasn't like I'd expected her to ask for world peace.

"You can talk to Mommy and Daddy about toys," I offered. "It's all right to ask God for those, but it's also nice to think of other people in our prayers. And sometimes we turn to God to help our hearts feel better."

From the rearview mirror, I saw her grin. "A Slinky would make me feel better."

I let the conversation end with hopes that my final words would be remembered, if not that moment, then someday.

The following week, her preschool had a holiday party, complete with a grab bag. Everyone threw in a gift and randomly pulled one out. When I arrived to take her home, my daughter ran toward me with obvious excitement.

"Mommy, look what I got!"

In her tiny hands, she held a box. On it was printed: "The Original Walking Spring Toy — Slinky."

Not even a cheap knock-off… it was the real deal.

Our conversation about prayer returned to me. It was probably just a coincidence, I thought, and pushed it from my mind.

But the Slinky tugged at me. Maybe it wasn't a coincidence. Maybe her prayers were heard, and next time she'd turn to God about something more significant, like helping her feel brave on her first day of kindergarten.

My next thought stopped me dead in my tracks. Was it possible that God had sent two messages that day? In the midst of my own doubts, could that entire scene have also been directed at me? And at that moment, I knew it had — a message that came in the form of a little metal toy.

It gave credence to the very words about prayer that I'd shared with my daughter. And ever since that moment, I've believed that my prayers have always been — and will continue to be — heard, too.

— Sharon A. Struth —

My Prayer

Dear God, thank you
for the wisdom of our children.
Through their innocence,
they often bring the lesson to the teacher.
Open my ears and my heart
so I can see you through them.
Amen.

54

No Ordinary Talk

*"I, even I, am he who blots out your transgressions,
for my own sake, and remembers your sins no more."*
~Isaiah 43:25

Late one night, I heard a gentle knock at my bedroom door. "Mom, are you asleep?" I struggled to wake up. Shawn's voice signaled distress.

"No, son. Come on in."

"Mom, I need to talk to you."

The last five months had been a test of wills between me and my high school senior. While my husband built our new retirement home in Arkansas, my job was to help Shawn finish out the school year successfully despite the throes of senioritis, a break-up with his girlfriend, and planning for his future.

My heart thumped in my chest as I waited while my six-foot-tall nineteen-year-old stretched his frame across my king-sized bed and began to pour out a confession. Straining to focus, I realized that my workday as a high-school principal would start in about four hours since I arose each day at 4:30. But I knew this was no ordinary talk and that my teenager was feeling the angst of his transition to maturity. He recited a myriad of wrongs he'd committed in the last few months and the lies he'd told us to cover them.

As the list grew, I realized that these might be normal behaviors for other seniors, but not for a youngster reared in our Christian home. My heart almost burst with the pain his admissions caused, but I kept silent and continued to listen. He ended with the crushing words, "Mom, I'm no longer a Christian. I've done so many bad things that I just can't claim that anymore."

God, help me find the words to deal with this, I prayed. And somehow He supplied them. "Son you are a Christian. We've raised you that way, and everything you've told me doesn't wipe that out. You've confessed your mistakes, and all we can do as Christians is to ask God's forgiveness. Everybody goes through something like this at times. We've all done things we're ashamed of, but that doesn't make God quit loving us."

"Are you sure? 'Cause I feel really bad about all this."

"I'm positive, honey. And what you've told me tonight is a good start."

He groped for my hand in the dark and clutched it. "Then pray for me," he sobbed.

I prayed as diligently as I had ever prayed in my life, wanting to jerk this mantle of guilt from my son's broad shoulders, but knowing he would have to wrestle his own way through it for a certain period of time. I realized that we mothers cannot fix every single thing in the universe. All we can do for our children is point the way.

More relaxed than when he first entered my bedroom, my son snuggled on the pillow next to mine. He continued to hold my hand and chattered non-stop about "normal" events until I became so sleepy I could no longer answer. Recognizing my need for sleep, he squeezed my hand and kissed me on the cheek. "I'm sorry I've kept you up so late. Thanks, Mom. You're the best."

Life seemed to become somewhat calmer for my anxious child after that night. The frenetic pace of the end-of-year events improved for both of us. I felt secure in the fact that God played a significant role in our restored relationship.

Two weeks before graduation, Shawn's life ended in a horrific automobile wreck caused by a drunk driver. Mothers often doubt their own counsel to their children, but when his friends testified of Shawn's example at his funeral, I knew my words had found their mark.

— Rita Billbe —

My Prayer

God, give us the right words as parents to make a difference in the lives of our children. Guide them to know we are always there for them, no matter how great the wrongs they have done.
Amen.

55

Waiting Room Prayers

Be joyful always; pray continually; give thanks
in all circumstances, for this is God's will
for you in Christ Jesus.
~1 Thessalonians 5:16-18

I quickly learned the telltale signs that my daughter, Taylor, was having another ear infection. Either she would wake up screaming in the middle of the night or start tugging on her ear during the day. Regardless of the symptoms, we would be off to the doctor for another check of her ears.

After suffering through seven ear infections, we were finally advised by her pediatrician to have small tubes inserted to help aid in the drainage of her ear canal. It was an outpatient surgery, but still required general anesthesia. It was the best decision for my little girl, but did not make me any less concerned. The potential for something to go wrong during surgery was still there.

On the morning of the operation, I spent some alone time with God. I asked Him to protect Taylor, and also guide her surgeon and those in the operating room. But it was still an excruciating moment when I had to release her into the arms of the waiting nurse. Even though they were all carefully trained professionals, they were not Mama. Time ticked slowly as I sat in the recovery room, waiting for any news of the operation and her prognosis.

During this time, I again went to God in prayer. But this time I started to pray for the other people in surgery and those nameless faces waiting with me in the sterile waiting room. Each of us had a sincere reason to worry. And as I prayed, a sense of peace and understanding eventually drifted over me. God was there that morning for me just as He was there for all the others. He is and always will be in every hospital, real or makeshift, in this world. He guides the hands of the doctors and nurses, cares for the injured, and brings peace to those worried and waiting. How great is His task! Yet, without fail, God is always there for us.

The surgery took a little longer than expected, but after an hour and a half, the surgeon finally came out with good news. The ear tubes had been inserted, her adenoids had been removed, and everything had gone smoothly. Taylor was a changed little girl after the surgery. It not only healed her ear infections, but cleared up the balance issues associated with her inner ear. At fourteen months, she had been crawling, but not walking. But after the surgery, she could finally stand and take her first steps.

Sometimes, prayer is the only way to get through those scary moments in our lives. All we can do is give it up to God and then trust. I now look at my daughter run across the room and know that she was the recipient of God's great gift of healing.

— Karen C. Talcott —

My Prayer

Dear Father, you truly know all the healing that we need in our bodies. Whether it is physical, mental, or emotional, guide us to the best care possible. But always help us to remember that you are the ultimate healer.
Amen.

56

A God of Second Chances

I call on you, O God, for you will answer me;
give ear to me and hear my prayer.
~Psalm 17:6

At last, bedtime! Time to put my two girls to sleep, make myself a cup of tea, and curl up on the couch with a good magazine. Tonight, I think I'll hurry things along—bath time can wait until tomorrow, and we can pick out some really short bedtime stories. A mother needs a break once in a while, right?

"Mama, this is Jesus. I think He is God's helper. Actually, He is just like God. Really, they are twins." Julia, my four-year-old, is lingering much too long over her children's Bible story.

"Yes, honey, Jesus is just like God. Now let's say our prayers and get to sleep." I close the Bible, trying not to feel too guilty for almost slamming it shut. (I need my warm cup of tea. My magazine is calling!)

"Our Father," my daughter prays, "deliver us from eagle, for dine is the kingdom, and the power, and the glory, forever and ever."

My heart melts a bit at my daughter's rendition of the Lord's Prayer. But I'd better get going. One kiss goodnight, and then it's tea time!

"Goodnight, sweetheart," I say, hastily pecking my daughter on the cheek.

But as I head toward the staircase, a glowing light peeks out from under my older daughter's door. Why isn't she asleep? All I want is some peace and quiet, and a nice warm cup of tea!

"Put the book away and go to sleep," I say, catching her reading a chapter book by flashlight. "Did you already say your prayers?"

"Yeah," she smiles, sheepishly clicking off her flashlight. "You know what?" she continues.

Why can't she hurry up this little conversation?

I cross my arms. "What is it?"

"Sometimes I pray at different times in the day, too. You don't just have to pray at bedtime, you know."

"When else do you pray?"

"Sometimes, I ask God to help me be good or brave. I don't always pray out loud, but God knows what's in your heart."

Yes, He does. Like when a mother is trying to rush bedtime and hurry through the important stuff in favor of a cup of tea.

"I love you," I say guiltily. Carefully, I take time to tuck in the covers and sneak an extra kiss. As I turn to leave, I see an open book on the nightstand—a children's devotional I'd been meaning to read to my daughter. The title? *Making Time for God.*

"Tomorrow night, let's start reading that book again," I say.

"Okay, Mama." My daughter's sweet smile tells me what I already know—God always gives second chances, even to harried, hurried mothers.

Later, as I linger over a cup of Earl Grey, I think about God's steady message of love, delivered through my children. What simple, unwavering faith. In my haste, I almost missed it.

— Stefanie Wass —

My Prayer

*Dear God, thank you for speaking through
the innocent, faithful voices of my children.
Help me to slow down and listen,
for they have so much to say.
Amen.*

57

Broken Bones and Prayers

When I am afraid, I will trust in you.
~Psalm 56:3

J uly 17, 2009, began like any other Friday. I went out to the barn to feed the animals, and then came back inside to get our daughter out of bed. My husband and four-year-old son hugged us goodbye as they left. Chris would drop Cody off at Grandma's house on his way to work. Cody always looked forward to Fridays with Grandma. They usually spent the morning playing in her kitchen or garden while I worked from home and cared for one-year-old Kayce.

On this particular morning, the phone rang unexpectedly as I was feeding Kayce her breakfast. It was Chris. In a tense voice, he told me there had been an accident at Grandma's house, and Cody was hurt. I pulled Kayce out of the highchair, and we jumped in the car.

Ten minutes later, I arrived to find Cody lying on the living room floor, crying and screaming. His left leg was grossly swollen, and his ribs had begun to turn black and blue. Beside him lay the grandfather clock that normally stood against the wall. The doors to the chime cabinet were open, and the glass face of the clock was shattered. That old, heavy clock had fallen on top of him.

As gently as possible, Grandma picked him up and placed him in the back of my SUV, climbing in beside Cody to support him. I took off for the nearest emergency room a half-hour away. I had never driven so fast in my life. Cody's cries frightened me.

When we arrived, a male nurse lifted Cody directly onto a gurney from the back of the SUV. The ER doctor barked orders to those around him. A short time later, we were given the news: Cody's left femur was badly fractured. X-rays vividly revealed the bone, now splintered at a forty-five-degree angle. My breath caught in my throat as Grandma broke down in tears.

A short time later, we met the orthopedic surgeon who would set the broken bone. He explained that, because of the severity of the break, Cody would need to be in a body cast for at least six weeks. As we walked alongside the gurney toward pre-op, I tried to hold back the tears. I was terrified that Cody had to be under anesthesia for the procedure. I silently begged the Lord to calm my pounding heart. Cody began to cry when the nurse told us we couldn't continue any farther with him. At that moment, I leaned over him and whispered in his ear the words of Psalm 56:3, "When I am afraid, I will trust in you." I repeated the verse several times to him and promised we would be there when he woke up.

The hour and a half in the waiting room felt like years. I spent the time silently repeating Psalm 56:3 over and over. Though anxious, my heart calmed. Cody came out of the anesthesia very well, and our focus turned to learning how to care for him in the body cast.

The next six weeks were a rollercoaster time of good news and bad, triumphs and setbacks, but through it all we gave our fears to the Lord in prayer. When Cody's cast came off, we faced the challenge of helping him learn to walk again, but we made it through by confidently trusting the Lord every day.

— Jenny R. George —

My Prayer

Dear Heavenly Father, thank you for your strength
of presence when circumstances beyond our control
shake our emotional foundations. You are an oasis
of courage when we are anxious and afraid.
Help us, Father, to always remember
to put our trust in you.
Amen.

58

Beautiful Day

*"My God sent his angel, and he shut the mouths
of the lions. They have not hurt me, because I was
found innocent in his sight. Nor have I ever done any
wrong before you, O king."*
~Daniel 6:22

I looked out the window to see a fluffy blanket of snow covering our neighborhood and icicles crowning each house. Despite the freezing temperatures, the bright sun lit up the winter sky. With my morning coffee in hand, I thanked God for protecting my family. I continued my daily meditation, knowing that it was going to be a beautiful day.

My ten-year-old son, Sean, was quite excited about the morning as well. He sat eagerly in front of the television set waiting to see the name of his school listed at the bottom of the screen, hoping for a snow day. When his school finally appeared, his excitement matched that of scoring the winning touchdown during the Super Bowl. There aren't too many things more exciting to a kid than a snow day. The next thing I knew, the phone was ringing, and Sean was making plans with his friends to play in the snow.

I had to laugh when I watched the boys walk out of the house in their winter gear. With two sweatshirts and a turtleneck, long underwear, pants, layers of socks and snow boots all under a heavy coat, Sean waddled away from the house like a seal.

What I didn't know was that the boys would soon be in danger. Despite their better judgment, they ended up at the pond. They decided to see if it was frozen enough for them to ride their bikes across, so Sean started walking on it to check it out. Slowly but surely, he inched out until he was rather far. Without warning, he fell completely through the ice.

Freezing cold and weighed down by all of his winter clothes, he attempted to tread water and keep his head afloat. But he could not get out alone, and his friends were unable to help him. Sean had only one thing left to do: he prayed. Suddenly, he felt a hand guide him as he was pushed up and out of the icy water and back to safety. The Lord was watching over him and sent His angels to rescue him.

Several weeks later, I learned the story of Sean's "close call" from his Sunday school teacher. Like most kids, even though this story has a happy ending, he was sure he would be in big trouble at home for playing at the pond. I wondered how many other times the Lord has stepped in to rescue our children that we haven't found out about.

As I begin my mornings with the Lord, I have a newfound gratitude for the very real way in which God protects his children. With my trust in the Lord, I know that every day is truly going to be a beautiful day.

— Karen Krokroskia as told to Angela N. Abbott —

My Prayer

Father, thank you for hearing our prayers and
sending your angels to rescue us. Help me to teach
my children to pray and trust in you so that when I
am not there, they will call out to you.
Thank you for being with us in our times of need.
Amen.

59

A Mother Knows Best

*"Again, I tell you that if two of you on earth agree
about anything you ask for, it will be done for you by
my Father in heaven. For where two or three come
together in my name, there am I with them."*
~Matthew 18:19-20

Two weeks before I was due to give birth to my fourth child, I began
to have nagging feelings that my little one would be stillborn. I
tried to brush off the worries as those of a neurotic mother, and,
for fear of looking silly, I did not mention my concerns to a soul.

The last few weeks of pregnancy were tedious, and in an effort
to occupy my time, I agreed to drive an hour to meet up with friends.
In the midst of all the chatter, my friend Chantal suddenly stopped
and announced, "I really feel that we all need to pray right now that
Michelle will have a safe delivery and a healthy baby." As my friends
flocked around me, my mind flashed to my recent fears, but I pushed
them aside again. In light of today's medical advances, stillbirth was
not exactly a common occurrence.

We had recently moved to a rural town, and our plan was to have
the baby at the small local hospital, rather than drive an hour to the

city and deliver at the large obstetrical teaching hospital. Although my previous labors had been long and drawn out, I was classified as low-risk with no foreseeable problems.

As my due date came and went, I decided to pay my old OB in the city one last visit, rather than go to my new local GP. I made the drive, where she delivered the disappointing news that nothing was happening down south and promised to see me again in a few days. As I began to drive to the city outskirts, contractions started out of the blue. Rather than following their usual meandering path, they came fast and furious, one minute apart and lasting for forty-five seconds each. While waiting for Craig, my husband, to leave work, I called Labor and Delivery at the city hospital. They told me that given my history and my recent doctor's appointment, it would likely die down, and not to feel any need to come in. But by the time Craig caught up with me, I felt uneasy. We decided to go in and get checked at L&D for peace of mind.

At L&D, the nurse checked me and declared that, despite the contractions, I was not in labor. They were discussing sending me home when suddenly I felt a gush. "Oh!" I groaned, half excited and half in pain. "I think my water just broke."

The nurse checked me, and her face went pale. "That's not your water, honey, that's blood."

The next ten minutes were a blur. I was raced into the operating room and prepped for a crash C-section as the little heartbeat disappeared from the monitor. As the anesthetic blacked me out, I breathed half a prayer for my baby's life.

When I awoke, my first thought was, "Dear God, they are going to tell me that my baby is gone." I struggled to open my eyes and caught sight of Craig sitting beside the bed holding a small white bundle.

"It's a boy," he whispered. "And he's okay!"

It turned out that my placenta had abrupted, cutting Timothy off from the vital oxygen he needed. Solely because we were at this particular hospital, steps away from the OR, my baby was alive. Had we followed everyone's advice to go home, my little Timothy would have been stillborn. I suddenly recalled my nagging feelings… and Chantal's intervening prayers.

— Michelle Peters —

My Prayer

*Dear God, thank you for answering our prayers
when we gather together, and for showing yourself in miraculous
ways. Help me to keep you forefront in my mind. It is a blessing
that I can bring to you every day not only my hopes, dreams,
worries and fears, but also those of the people I care about.
Amen.*

60

An Angel in the Woods

Do not forget to entertain strangers,
for by so doing some people have
entertained angels without knowing it.
~Hebrews 13:2

How could this happen? We had turned our backs for just a moment, and now our seven-year-old daughter was lost in the Colorado forest.

Our family was on vacation and had stopped to admire a thunderous waterfall, loud and large due to the summer snowmelt. A dirt trail led up from the parking lot to the overlook, and we had walked the half-mile to view the magnificent mountain water scene. While we admired the view, our daughter wandered away. The forest ranger walked down to the station to see about forming a search party while I quickly hiked to the truck. Along the way, I prayed that our daughter had simply grown bored and returned to the vehicle. My husband stayed above, his mind racing. Neither of us dared voice our greatest fear that perhaps she had fallen into the gorge below.

My husband walked a short distance along the trail and came to a fork. That's when he saw the dog. A stray, male black Lab that had followed us from the parking lot to the overlook stood at the fork, his nose pointing in the direction opposite the parking lot. The ranger had said earlier that the dog adopted a new group of trail walkers each day, and this time he'd chosen us. Now, the dog's eyes were watching the forest, ears forward as if listening. My husband listened, too. Then he heard our daughter's voice, yelling: "I'm lost! Someone help me! Mommy, Daddy, can you hear me? I'm lost!"

Together, my husband and the dog ran along the path that shortly ended but showed trampled grass. After a moment, my husband encouraged the dog, "Find her, boy! Find my little girl!"

That's the command the Lab seemed to need. He plunged into the dark woods, with my husband quickly following. Within twenty minutes, our little girl was wrapped tightly in his arms, and the three of them walked back to the waterfall observation station where other hikers, the ranger, and I were huddled, planning a search. As I held my young child, she cried and said, "I'm sorry! I tried to get to the truck and went the wrong way, I guess. I couldn't find the truck. I couldn't find you."

"The dog found her," my husband said tearfully, and hugged the wonderful rescue dog. "He heard her, and he helped me find her."

The ranger patted the dog's head and said in amazement, "He just showed up a few days ago and hangs around. We've wondered where he came from. But maybe this is why he's here."

As my husband held our girl again, I knelt beside the dog. I petted his wide black head and looked into his eyes. Those kindly brown eyes never wavered from mine, as if reassuring me he was the answer God gave to my prayer of finding our daughter. The Lord says in Ezekiel 34:16, "I will search for the lost and bring back the strays." This stray dog searched for and found my lost little girl and returned her safely to our family.

Maybe that's why my daughter loves dogs to this day. She will tell you that she believes some dogs are angels sent by God for a purpose—just like that black Lab on a hiking trail in Colorado that the ranger called "a stray."

A stray? Maybe. An angel? We think so. A coincidence? We don't believe that for a minute!

— Marcia Mansfield as told to Gayle Irwin —

My Prayer

Lord, thank you for searching for those who are lost. Help us to remember that whenever we give help or are helped by strangers, perhaps you've set them in our path for a purpose. Your grace, provision, love, and kindness are unmatched.
In Jesus' name, we give you praise.
Amen.

61

Why Didn't I Think of That?

"If you believe, you will receive whatever you ask for in prayer."
~Matthew 21:22

When my oldest daughter, Kaylee, was five, my three younger children attended a "Mom's Day Out" program at our church. This allowed Kaylee and me to spend two whole mornings a week together—just the two of us. Yellow buses, lunchboxes, and Kaylee's first pair of school shoes were just around the corner, so I planned our days carefully. I hoped to show Kaylee God's presence in her life before I had to send her off to kindergarten. We filled our time with walks through trees ablaze in fall colors. We took trips to the zoo, where we discovered new facts about God's creation. We even handed out homemade valentines at a nursing home.

Our house was thirty miles from town, on three lush acres, situated atop a hill overlooking the entire county. Kaylee and I spent many of our mornings enjoying that view from the rocking chairs on our wraparound porch. After one morning, we were getting ready to pick up my younger kids from "Mom's Day Out" when I realized my keys were missing. I usually kept my keys in my van in the garage because keeping keys inside the house was way too risky. My younger boys, like the raccoons in our woods, were fascinated with shiny objects. I had previously rescued my keys from a heater vent, a sandbox, and even the dreaded toilet. Since my keys were not in the van, I assumed my boys had discovered them.

Kaylee and I looked everywhere, but my keys were officially lost. Panic-stricken, I called our church and told them I was going to be late picking up the kids. After I got off the phone, possible solutions raced through my mind. My husband was out of town, so he was no help. I didn't have neighbors near enough to give us a ride. Even if I did, I couldn't ask them to drive half an hour each way. I was considering a taxi when Kaylee's voice broke through my thoughts.

"Mama, the only thing left to do is pray."

"Why didn't I think of that?" I thought to myself.

We held hands, and she prayed six simple words: "Dear God, please fix this. Amen."

When she lifted her head, there was a twinkle in her big brown eyes.

"Mom," she said, "what about the old red truck?"

I explained to her that we had the keys to it, but that really didn't matter because it hadn't run in a long time. She insisted that we try it anyway. I figured it wouldn't hurt to test it, even though I was sure it wouldn't start. We headed across the field and climbed in the truck. I turned the key. The truck sputtered, spit, and then — died. Kaylee begged me to try again, only this time she wanted to pray first.

"God," she said, "we really need you to fix this. Amen."

I smiled and turned the key. The truck sputtered, spit, and then — started! I was so surprised that I laughed out loud.

Kaylee squealed, "I knew it! I knew He could fix anything, Mom." Believe it not, that rusty old truck got us all the way to town and back.

I still laugh when I think about that day. Despite all my plans, it was Kaylee, with her childlike faith, who showed me just how near God really is.

— Leah Clancy —

| Help from Above

My Prayer

Thank you, Lord, for your continual presence in our lives. Please bless us with child-like faith and remind us that you are ready and willing to "fix" anything we ask you to.
Amen.

62

God Sent His Angels

For he will command his angels concerning
you to guard you in all your ways.
~Psalm 91:11

I t had been a normal pregnancy, but as I waited for the late afternoon doctor's appointment, I was worried. On the phone, the
nurse had assured me that it was probably nothing, but I knew
something was not right.

Later, as I saw the concern on the doctor's face, my worst fears
were confirmed. Although I was only at thirty-two weeks and feeling
no contractions, I was in labor. The doctor sent me straight to the
hospital. Five hours later, our son was born. Despite his early arrival
and low birth weight of only three pounds, nine ounces, the doctor
assured us that he was healthy. We were thrilled with our new arrival!
However, reality set in the next morning when we were escorted to
the neonatal intensive care unit and saw our tiny baby lying in the
incubator. The steady beat of monitors and countless wires coming
from his body were not reassuring. Holding him in my arms, I was
keenly aware of how small he was.

The next few days became a blur. I left the hospital with empty
arms. The days turned into weeks, and the constant trips to the hospital

became exhausting. When I wasn't at the hospital, I was tense each time the phone rang, fearing it would be the hospital with bad news.

Fear and depression plagued me. My heart pleaded with God to let our son live. I also asked for strength to make it through each day. I pictured an angel standing at each corner of my baby's incubator. Peace flooded my heart, and I was able to rest in the assurance that even though I could not always be with my son, God was always present, and He would send His angels to guard my little one.

After three-and-a-half weeks, the ordeal finally ended. Our son had gained enough weight to go home. We were overjoyed! In His love and faithfulness, God had answered my prayer.

Our son graduates from college next year. I've never forgotten those angels who guarded his incubator. I'm sure they have come to his aid many times. As much as I love my son, my love can never compare to the great love God has for His children. He knows our deepest longing and will always be there to meet our needs.

Oh, I almost forgot. Our son's first day home was Mother's Day!

— Karen Asire —

My Prayer

Dear Father, thank you for offering
your compassion during our times of need. Your
faithfulness and love are beyond our understanding.
May we daily live in the reality of your presence.
Amen.

63

Stranger or Angel?

The LORD protects the simplehearted;
when I was in great need, he saved me.
~Psalm 116:6

It was the middle of the afternoon, and Chris was playing outside at the apartment complex into which we had recently moved. Billy needed a nap, and I needed someone to care about me—I felt hopeless and alone.

Divorce is such a big, ugly, destructive word. I had failed at everything. Marriage. Giving two little guys a secure family life. I had married young and didn't prepare for anything but being a wife and mother. That was my only ambition, and I wanted to be good at both. Now that was a shattered dream.

"I feel like I'm wearing a big 'L' on my forehead for loser," I sobbed into the phone.

My friend Marilyn assured me it wasn't true, but she was just being kind.

Chris was six, and Billy was a year old. Life was one big obstacle course, and I had these two precious children to care for.

"Jan, God knew you were going to go through this, and He's got a plan. Just trust Him."

That was okay for Marilyn to say. She was married to a very successful man, had a wonderful family, and was a leader in the community. Her family had been named "Family of the Year" by the local newspaper the year before.

"Just trust Him. He'll take care of you," she repeated as we said goodbye.

I hung up the phone feeling no better than I had before. If God loved me so much, why was I going through so much pain, and feeling so alone and afraid? These two little boys were dependent on me, and I was clueless about how I could take care of them even though I loved them with every cell in my body.

I picked up Billy and put him in bed for a nap, then kissed his little upturned, smiling face. Both boys had such trust it scared me. Their lives were in my hands.

The front door opened, and Chris walked in soaking wet, tears streaming down his face.

"Son, what happened?"

"A kid pushed me in the pool." He stood looking up at me, waiting for my reaction.

"What?" The apartment complex sprawled over several acres on top of a hill. I put my arms around him and pulled him close. "How'd it happen?"

"I was talking to this kid by the pool, and he just pushed me into the deep end."

My mind whirled. Chris couldn't swim.

"How did you get out of the water?" My body trembled, but I tried not to get hysterical in front of him.

"A man jumped in and saved me. He told me, 'You're a lucky boy. If I hadn't forgotten something and come back to get it, you'd be dead. There's nobody home 'round here 'cause everybody works in this quadrangle.' Isn't that somethin', Mom?"

I sank into a nearby chair, weak with relief, but now my tears were tears of joy. Yes, it was something. It was just as Marilyn had said: God knew Chris would get pushed into the pool, and He sent a stranger — or an angel — to save him. I wasn't alone. It was the sign

I needed that God would help me raise these precious little boys. He alone is the perfect Father.

— Jan Brand —

My Prayer

Lord, thank you for sending your loving helpers
into our lives and the lives of our children.
So often, you know our needs
before we have even uttered our fears out loud.
Please continue to watch over our beloved children
and keep them safe from earthly dangers.
Amen.

64

The Power of Prayer

*I lift up my eyes to the hills — where does my help
come from? My help comes from the LORD,
the Maker of heaven and earth.*
~Psalm 121:1-2

It was the phone call every parent dreads.

"Mom, I was in a car accident today. I'm in the campus hospital but I'm all right."

But our daughter wasn't all right, the nurse informed us.

"There's internal bleeding. She's injured her pelvis and spleen. It would be best if you come as soon as possible."

Driving over the Blue Ridge Mountains in the inky darkness, my husband tightly gripped the steering wheel. Silently, I prayed next to him.

"Please, Lord, be with our daughter. We love her so much…." A sob escaped from somewhere inside.

Paralyzed with fear and worry, those few words were all I could muster. Fortunately I'd telephoned prayer warriors around the country, asking them to pray on our behalf.

The following days were touch-and-go as our daughter received blood transfusions and pain medication. I remained at the hospital with her, sometimes curled up in a ball on the edge of her bed, both of us entwined in IV apparatus.

Then something unusual occurred. The sterile, antiseptic-smelling hospital experienced a metamorphosis of sorts as college students began sneaking into our daughter Autumn's private hospital room. The "No Visitors" sign was ignored as they quietly gathered around her, guardian angels in the night, praying or softly singing, asking God to heal their friend. The stark-looking cement walls of the hospital room became transformed as well as these same angels completely covered them with cheerful artwork, humorous cartoons, and reassuring Bible verses.

The doctor informed us that our daughter would need additional surgery on her spleen. While friends visited, I escaped to the hospital chapel for a moment of solitude. My husband would be joining us when he got off work, making the long trek over the mountains once again.

But, for now, I was alone.

"Please, Lord, I'm so overwhelmed I can't find the words to pray! I love you. Help me to trust you with our daughter's life!"

Silence answered. I turned to leave the chapel. A woman dressed in white guarded the door.

"Your daughter is going to be okay. Others are praying on your behalf."

Before I could reply, she disappeared out the chapel door and around a corner.

I hurried after her, only to find the hallways empty.

The mysterious woman was right. The surgery was successful. Two weeks later, our daughter slowly made her way across a dandelion-covered lawn at James Madison University to receive her teaching degree.

Autumn wasn't the only one who'd been learning, however. My husband and I had also learned a lesson or two. We learned to never doubt the power of intercessory prayer.

There will be times when burdens are too heavy to bear alone.

That's when God sends his angels to lighten the load… earthly and heavenly ones.

— Mary Z. Smith —

My Prayer

Father, there are times when we can't pray for ourselves because the burden is just too overwhelming. Thank you for sending your angels to intercede for us in our times of need.
Amen.

65

A Penny in My Palm

In my distress I called to the LORD; I
called out to my God. From his temple he
heard my voice; my cry came to his ears.
~2 Samuel 22:7

Giovanni sat in my lap and turned the large pages of his picture book, pointing and babbling happily. I rested my nose against the light, airy fuzz of his hair and breathed in his soft smell of baby shampoo and breakfast's yogurt. His round little cheeks were perfect, and his delicate eyelashes curled just right around his little hazel eyes. I stroked the top of his small fingernail, absorbing his perfection in the way only an adoring mother can.

Suddenly, emotion flooded my heart in a way I had never experienced. My heart started racing, and I felt my hands become clammy and shaky. What was wrong with me? Why was I panicking? I put Giovanni down on the carpet next to me and stood up. I had an instinct to pick him up again and never let him go. The only thought I could focus clearly on was that I needed to pray for Giovanni. *God, protect my son. Protect him physically and spiritually.* I picked up Giovanni and held him tightly, praying deeply with a love that is stronger than spoken words.

My usually wiggly toddler stayed still in my arms for almost ten minutes as I held him. The panic faded, and I found myself rocking him peacefully, tears drying on my cheeks. What was that all about? Unsure of what had happened, and embarrassed about the uncharacteristic frenzy of tears I had displayed, I kept the occurrence to myself. The rest of the day, however, I remained puzzled by the strength of what I had felt.

Late that same night, when I returned from work, I found my husband, Franklin, watching TV with an ashen expression. I knew in a moment that something serious had happened. He turned off the TV and told me to sit down. He took a shaky breath and started to speak. "Giovanni choked on a penny. I got it out. He is fine, and he is sleeping upstairs." I let out a long breath.

Franklin told me how he had found Giovanni gagging and tried to give him CPR. Nothing helped. Giovanni's bloodshot eyes bulged, he started turning blue, and his body went limp. He hit Giovanni violently on the back, but it did nothing. Something told him to try fishing the object out with his finger, and he did. He stuck his finger all the way to the bottom of Giovanni's throat, and Giovanni arched his back with the pain. He felt something. Franklin hooked his knuckle around the object and yanked it out, hoping desperately not to tear Giovanni's little throat. Instinctively, he knew the only other choice would be to watch his son die. Giovanni began coughing and scream- ing. Color returned to his face. Franklin looked down and saw a single wet penny in his palm.

Giovanni's choking dominated my thoughts over the following days, but I did not recognize the connection between my earlier emotional experience and his choking until my mom came to visit a few days later. She had not yet heard about the incident, but as soon as she walked through our door, she picked him up right away and hugged him tightly, whispering to him that he was an angel. I heard her and asked, "What are you talking about, Mom?" She hesitantly told me that she had dreamt Giovanni had been very close to death. It had been so realistic that she had woken up in a panic and was unable to return to sleep all night. She had the dream the night before Giovanni had choked.

Chills ran up and down my body as I listened to her story. When she finished, I told her that Giovanni had actually choked that night, and that I had experienced an urgent rush to pray for him that morning. With an overwhelming sense of gratitude, I understood that the prayer surging through my heart that morning may have had an actual effect on the survival of my son. I had been given the rare gift of experiencing the power that prayer emits in its purest form—a mother's love.

— Mary Delgado —

My Prayer

Heavenly Father, thank you for protecting our children and keeping them safe.
They may encounter many things in this life that could cause them harm, but remind me that you are ever present in those moments.
Amen.

66

The Little Green Book

For God did not give us a spirit of timidity,
but a spirit of power, of love and of self-discipline.
~2 Timothy 1:7

Considering I had never broken a bone, been stung by a bee, or even had one thread stitched through me, the delivery of my son was a terrifying event—but not just physically. I was also burdened by worry. That first night in the hospital, I stood alone in the gray-blue bathroom listening to my sobs echoing my child's. Why wouldn't he stop crying? How would I get him to eat? What would I do with him when I get home? When would I feel like me again?

These questions and more baffled me, especially since I thought I was more than prepared for Jay's arrival. After all, my husband and I had decorated his nursery, attended showers thrown in our honor, completed a series of birthing classes, and read just about every best-selling baby book on the shelves. Our baby would be the happiest on the block, and we would certainly be baby-wise! Yet there was one book I had not consulted very often throughout my pregnancy, and I needed it more than ever.

While still hiding away in that bathroom, with tears streaming down my cheeks and not knowing where to turn, I suddenly remembered the tiny green Bible I had stashed inside my overnight bag. A man had been handing out free copies of the pocket-sized book on the campus where I teach just the week before. When my water had broken unexpectedly, I began throwing movies, snacks, and clothes into a duffel. Before zipping up, I saw the little book sitting on the counter beside a stack of mail and thought it might come in handy. Little did I know it should have been at the top of my "To Pack" list.

Under the glare of the hospital bathroom's fluorescent lights, I turned to the table of contents. Inside was a reference to key verses for various emotions. It took me some time to pinpoint my feeling, but I knew for certain what to call it when I saw the word "Afraid."

As I read 2 Timothy 1:7, I vowed to rely upon the power of the Holy Spirit that I had forgotten lay within me. I dried my tears and went to the side of my son's bassinet, marveling at the miracle before me. And even though Jay was crying hysterically, my heart's gates finally opened wide enough to allow back in all the love and wonder I had been feeling those nine months prior whenever we heard his heartbeat or watched him twist and turn within my belly. Remembering the words I had just read, I took a deep breath and called in the nurse to give us guidance on how to soothe our precious little one. Within a half-hour, calm had returned.

After that evening, there were and continue to be times when I feel just as clueless and frightened. Simply going grocery shopping for the first time nearly brought me to tears! But instead of shutting myself away in the bathroom to cry, I remind myself to turn to that dog-eared page in the little green book that now rests in Jay's nursery. It is then that I remember the most powerful resource is right at my fingertips.

— Shannon Griffin Blair —

My Prayer

*Father, fill me with the mighty Holy Spirit during
times of uncertainty as a new mother.
Replace my anxieties with confidence and
the knowledge that you have not given me anything
more than I can handle.
Amen.*

67

Overcoming Bad Days

Peace I leave with you; my peace I give you.
I do not give to you as the world gives.
Do not let your hearts be troubled
and do not be afraid.
~John 14:27

One warm morning when my twins were toddlers, I removed their pajamas and placed their little diapered bodies in their indoor play-yard with some toys while I went into the next room for a moment. At first, upon noticing it was strangely quiet, I smiled in satisfaction, thinking that the twins were playing together nicely. But then I realized that it was just *too quiet* for my rambunctious boys. Usually, I could hear babbling, squeaking toys, and crying as one twin hit the other with a toy. It was too early for them to have fallen asleep. So, this sudden lack of noise indicated a definite problem. I tiptoed out to peek at the boys.

I recoiled in horror as my eyes took in the nauseating sight. I pleaded with God, *Please don't let that be what I think it is....* But it was. A discarded diaper lay on the floor, and sticky green poop was smeared everywhere! It was literally on every surface within the boys' reach—on their bodies, on the floor, and on all the toys. I was stunned.

What did I ever do to deserve this, Lord? I sank to the floor in defeat. Suddenly realizing I had to move quickly before the situation deteriorated further, I tearfully gathered up enough energy to pull everything out of the play-yard. I grabbed one boy under the arms and, trying to position him as far away from my body as possible, hauled him off to the shower. Nevertheless, despite my precautions, I looked down at one point to find green slime smeared all over me, too! I stripped down to my underwear (praying that the doorbell wouldn't ring), showered my little mischief-maker, and returned to the other room to take care of his brother.

With both boys finally clean and ready to be dressed, I reached for the clean diapers. As I turned to rejoin the twins, I saw one of them peeing all over the floor! *How much worse could this get?* I diapered the boys, scrubbed the floor, and managed to get everyone dressed. I was nearing the finish line. The last items to be tackled were the poopy toys and clothes I'd thrown out of the play-yard. Picking up the dirty diaper from the floor, I discovered it was swarming with ants! Apparently, when I'd thrown it out of the play-yard, it had landed near the window and lured a colony of ants in for breakfast. I rushed the diaper out to the trashcan in the garage, cleaned up as many ants as I could find, and finally collapsed on the couch. I then proceeded to unload a few more choice words on God.

Okay, God, I fumed, *you've tested my patience enough today. Please pick on somebody else!* Thankfully, the rest of the day went much more smoothly. At long last, it was bedtime. Before joining my husband on the couch, I sidled up to the cribs to check on our little guys. They looked so sweet and innocent in their sleepers. Their soft blond hair curled around their heads as their tiny hands gripped their stuffed animals. They were peacefully asleep. *Dear God,* I whispered once again, *what did I ever do to deserve this?* It must have been something very good, I realized, as I breathed a prayer of thanksgiving.

— Susan M. Heim —

My Prayer

Dear Father, help me to remember that your blessings outweigh any trials I may go through. What a joy it is to be a mother, even when dirty diapers and ants complicate the day. Thank you for the wisdom of hindsight and a sense of humor! Amen.

68

Worry or Pray

Cast all your anxiety on him because he cares for you.
~1 Peter 5:7

My little boy sat all alone in one corner of the pre-K classroom. His red-rimmed eyes and swollen nose told the story of his day at school—another day spent in tears.

Too young to write words, he was making pictures of everything he'd done that day. When a teacher attempted to throw away some of his many scribbled papers, he cried, "No, don't take them! I might forget to tell Mommy and Daddy about something I did today."

A bell halted the frenzy of crayon on paper. In moments, he'd have to put on his coat to go out for recess, but suddenly he couldn't resist an urge to tap his cheek and count the repetitions. His stomach ached, and he wanted to go home. He'd skipped lunch when he saw the broken crackers on the tray—evidence to him that someone might have taken a bite from his lunch.

When the three o'clock bell rang, he tried to remember how to pack his backpack in the exact order he did yesterday and the day before that. Perhaps that would make everything all right.

At home, this inner conflict continued. He hardly touched his supper. "See these animal shapes in the chicken, Mom? I can't eat those."

"Try this then." I pointed at his macaroni and cheese.

"Are there germs in it?"

After supper, he played with his toys, but used only his smallest finger to touch them. The rest of his hand coiled in a tight fist. That week, the preschool teacher called me, concerned about his actions at school. I wasn't sure what was happening, but I knew we needed to see our pediatrician.

When Austin was diagnosed with obsessive compulsive disorder at age five, I had so many questions. Did I do something to cause this? Would he ever be "normal?" Why us? It broke my heart to see a little boy with so much anxiety. It hurt my pride that I couldn't make it better.

Austin was placed on medication, and we saw a therapist who taught him how to "boss back the worries" when they came. During one of those sessions, the doctor asked him, "What should we do when we have worries?"

"We pray and ask Jesus to take them away."

I grinned. I'm sure the therapist expected Austin to respond with one of the techniques he'd learned, but in simple understanding he demonstrated that we should turn to Jesus first. His faith inspired me and reminded me that God was present, even in the counseling room.

Scripture tells us to have faith like a child. Think about that. A child believes that God can do anything. In simple faith, Austin demonstrated the principle from 1 Peter 5:7 — to cast all our anxiety on God because He cares for us. It's so easy for moms to worry. We have plenty to worry about! But God asks us to give it to Him because He loves us and is able to bear our burdens.

By the end of second grade, Austin was off all medication, and he hasn't seen a therapist in more than seven years. I praise God for healing him, and I'm so grateful for what I learned in the process. God can handle my worries. He can handle yours, too.

— Michelle Rayburn —

My Prayer

Sovereign God, help me to let go of my anxiety and rest in your ability to see the road ahead.
Thank you for loving me and caring for my every need. Teach me how to be an example of faith to my children as I trust in you.
Amen.

69

You Don't Know It All

*"For my thoughts are not your thoughts,
neither are your ways my ways,"
declares the LORD. "As the heavens are
higher than the earth, so are my ways
higher than your ways and my thoughts
than your thoughts."
~Isaiah 55:8-9*

If you had asked me to write a parenting book before Nikki arrived, I would have shared my vast knowledge and wisdom on how to raise children. After all, I was a mom with three children who were fairly well behaved. But with this baby girl, I found that most of my old parenting knowledge and skills did not work.

On November 16, 2004, a little girl entered our world. All of our other children were blond and blue-eyed and resembled me. This little girl had brown hair, green eyes, and looked exactly like her dad. She had her own schedule, which constantly changed. She ran the show. She marched to the tune of a different drummer. I have cleaned up toothpaste, sugar, flour, powder, gel, shampoo, Vaseline, and any other product you can think of smeared everywhere. When it is quiet, my heart pounds, and I know something bad is happening. Our four cats run in sheer terror as she chases them to catch one to "pet." Somehow she manages to give our dog just enough love for him to put up with her crawling all over him.

Nikki has taught me more about parenting than any of my other three children. She demands that I parent her. She will not be babysat by the TV. She does not enjoy toys. She wants activity, activity, and more activity. She runs at full-speed all day, and yet every night, my husband and I lovingly look at this little bundle of energy that has fallen asleep for a very brief six to seven hours. You can't help but love her, knowing that she is something special.

I wanted to be the perfect mother, but I felt like a failure when I had Nikki. But one of my mentors told me that he has never met a mom who thinks she is a wonderful mom. We are very hard on ourselves. While we can never achieve God's perfection, we can model our parenting after Him—the ultimate parent. When I really started looking into it, I realized the main ingredient to being a great mom is unconditional love. Loving my children no matter what naturally comes easy. All the other stuff is just a bonus.

God chose me to be the parent of Brett, Nolan, Shelby, and Nikki. He placed these children in my womb and selected me to be their mother. That insight helps me to comprehend that God is a perfectionist in matchmaking. He has given me the skills and talents I need to raise these specific children.

I will never be perfect, but I am the perfect mother for them.

— Michelle Rocker —

My Prayer

Dear Lord, thank you for choosing me to be my children's mother. Help me to trust in you when I feel the need for perfection in my life. Each of my children comes with unique talents, and it is my hope that I am always aware of these gifts.need. Teach me how to be an example of faith to my children as I trust in you.
Amen.

70

In His Arms

> *The eternal God is your refuge, and underneath*
> *are the everlasting arms.*
> *~Deuteronomy 33:27*

My baby is choking!" my panicked voice cried as I tightly squeezed the nurse's call button. Mesmerized, my husband and I had been gazing at our two-day-old son, Andrew, while he slumbered. Suddenly, he began to kick his legs and spew frothy saliva from his lips. My husband grabbed Andrew to run with him to the nurses' station, but two nurses reacted to my call and met us at our hospital door. Both my husband and a nurse gave Andrew hard pats on the back to stop his choking. He immediately stopped struggling, relaxed, and breathed easily. The mysterious choking was baffling. Nothing was found to be wrong with our healthy, full-term newborn, and we were discharged from the hospital just hours later.

I had given birth to my son two days before, but it was in those few terrifying seconds while he choked that I became a parent. The cocoon of peaceful bliss that surrounded my heart was pierced with worry and fear, and a multitude of questions ricocheted through my mind. What if we hadn't been there when Andrew's episode had started? What if he did it again? From how many other dangers must I protect him?

Surrendering Our Worries | 193

Our first night home was a sleepless one for me. I stayed up, checking on my son in his crib until, exhausted, I fell asleep on the couch near daybreak, my ear glued to the baby monitor. The next day at Andrew's checkup, I told his doctor that I hadn't slept and why.

"You can't keep doing that," he said of my lack of sleep. He tried to reassure me that Andrew would be all right. But that was hard for me to accept. Andrew was so little and helpless. I had to protect him. I felt the responsibility weigh heavily on my shoulders, and my heart was burdened.

And then some sage words from a mom of three in my Sunday school class came back to me. She had imparted some of her wisdom to me before I started my own journey of motherhood.

"Children are a gift from God," she said. "They do not belong to us; they are entrusted to us by God for a little while."

I thought of Hannah from the Bible. She was able to give her young son, Samuel, back to God at the tabernacle and rejoice. She realized, as did my friend, that children are a gift from the Lord. It was hard for me to accept that ultimately I wasn't the one in control; I can't save Andrew the way God can. As his earthly mother, my responsibility is to teach him that his Heavenly Father is sovereign. Is there any guarantee that he will be safe from all the dangers that sometimes enter my imaginative mind? Not in this imperfect, fallen world. Andrew's spiritual protection is what will matter for eternity, and the only place that security can be found is in the everlasting arms of God. That is where I must place him, along with my worries.

When I turn my fears over to God, I stop turning and tossing at night. Only in His arms can my heart truly be wrapped in a cocoon of blissful peace.

— Janeen Lewis —

My Prayer

Dear God, help me to put my trust in you to protect my child and calm my fears. When my thoughts stray to places of darkness, help me to turn back to your pure light and truth. Thank you for the precious gift of motherhood, and I ask you to grant me the wisdom to be a good mother.

Amen.

71

Sunday Was My Day of Rest

*For six days, work is to be done,
but the seventh day is a Sabbath of rest,
holy to the Lord.*
~Exodus 31:15

I still remember it clearly. We were invited to attend a twins/multiples club summer picnic. I knew I was feeling overwhelmed with the amount of work that goes into raising twin babies, and I hoped to get some words of advice from other mothers. As we ate our lunch, I couldn't help glancing over at a very overwhelmed new mother. She was a mother of eight-week-old triplets. She had a baby on each hip, and was rocking the third in the stroller with her foot.

After a few moments, I asked her where her husband was. She pointed across the playground to a man chasing down an energetic toddler boy. My heart went out to her immediately. She told me about the challenges of raising three babies and her young son while her husband worked. I was a mess just trying to manage my own household and could not fathom what her life must have been like.

The demanding schedule of the twins and the needs of my two-and-a-half-year-old daughter were always in the forefront of my mind. I was tired, crying all the time, and struggling to stay afloat. Did I have postpartum depression? Maybe, but I didn't have time to treat it. My days and nights were a constant blur of feedings, diapers, and chaos. My husband tried to help in the evenings, but I was also feeling bitter. I felt that his life was easier than mine because he got to go off to work each day. At least he left the house, took a shower, and talked to adults. Meanwhile, I stayed home and cared for the needs of the babies while sorely neglecting mine.

Looking back on that time, I can say that the only place that truly existed as a refuge was church. We attended a contemporary service each Sunday. The service had a relaxed feel to it, and families were encouraged to attend. My husband and I often sat in the back row with our infant twins in our arms and listened to the word of God. As the twins grew, we eventually put them in the nursery. We cherished this one hour with God each Sunday. For the first time all week, I felt that I could be an adult. I could sing praise songs and listen to the sermon without distractions. I lived for Sundays!

And to this day, that feeling has never subsided. As the children grew, we all grew in our faith. This is a cherished time for our family. It is never a question whether we are going to church; it is always a given. God offers His house of worship to anyone who needs a place of solace. During the first year, I clung to my faith and my church. I moved in a blur six days a week, but on the seventh day, I was able to rest.

— Karen C. Talcott —

My Prayer

Dear God, there are times in my life when I feel so inadequate to cope. I know that you are there to help and bring me peace. Guide me back to you so that I may always lay my worries at your feet and feel your loving arms around me
Amen.

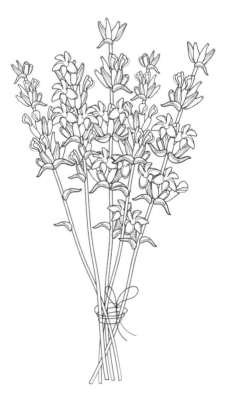

72

I'm Somebody's Mom

He restores my soul. He guides me in paths
of righteousness for his name's sake.
~Psalm 23:3

Motherhood had not come easily. With a thorny fertility issue and a difficult miscarriage behind me, I had ignored the advice of seasoned moms who had warned against hospital "rooming in for baby and mom."

You see, my maternal love affair had commenced nine months earlier. This was not a fetus, a mere cluster of continually dividing cells I was carrying. This was a baby, my baby—God's gift—and I was determined to get to know him. Gregarious by nature, I had commenced introductions as I departed my first prenatal checkup, telling the child beneath my heart all about his mom and dad.

I spoke daily of the hopes and dreams we held for him, but most importantly, of how we longed to watch him follow his own path, his own dreams. Similarly, I took his cues, provided by quickening, tumbling, and kicking, as little snapshots into his personality—this was one busy guy I was carrying! So, how could I allow anyone or anything to separate me from the child I had waited so long to hold in my arms?

Little did I realize the toll that nursing and a C-section would take. Thus, by the second night in the hospital, I readily accepted the recommendation made by an experienced RN in the newborn unit: "Let me bring Kevin to the nursery around midnight and give you a few hours of uninterrupted sleep. He'll be fine, and I promise to bring him to you when it's time for the next feeding." Could those seasoned moms have been right all along?

As the hour of separation drew near, I found myself filled with apprehension. With tears welling, I handed my precious bundle over to a woman who had cared for thousands of babies during her three-decade tenure on the maternity floor. And yet I asked: Would she take good care of my baby? Had I made the right decision to choose a little sleep over "rooming in?" Had mother-guilt set in already?

Soon, I woke to a gentle nudge. "I'm sorry to bother you, Mrs. Nichols. I've tried everything—rocking, sugar water, walking, singing—all to no avail. I know Kevin isn't hungry; he nursed well for you. I'm convinced that he misses you and needs to hear your voice."

Did she really say that my newborn son actually missed me, that he recognized my voice? The nurse placed my sobbing seven-pound miracle in my arms. As I held him close, he gazed briefly into my eyes while I reassured him that all was well, that I loved him. He then fell into a deep, restful sleep.

There are many defining "mother moments," but none more profound than the minute I realized that my child needed me to provide his care and comfort. I was somebody's mom—Kevin's mom. What an awesome responsibility God had given me, and what a journey it has been.

— Janice Flood Nichols —

My Prayer

Dear God, help me to be the mother that my child deserves—to know when to hold tight and when to let go, when to speak up and when to remain silent. I know I will stumble, but let me accept with grace that I am only my child's keeper, that the care and comfort I offer with love is merely a launch pad.
Amen.

73

Harsh Words

Get rid of all bitterness, rage and anger,
brawling and slander, along with every
form of malice. Be kind and compassionate
to one another, forgiving each other,
just as in Christ God forgave you.
~Ephesians 4:31-32

It's hard to admit, even now, but I did it! In one moment of extreme frustration over my son's behavior, I said all the things I swore I'd never say, used words I swore I'd never use. I felt them coming and should have run and locked myself away until they passed. But anger and frustration built, and out they came, cresting the bank of self-control and flooding over our day.

As the mother of children with special needs, there were often challenges that tried us all. But until that day, I had done a reasonable job of keeping anxiety and annoyance at bay. I tried to be my children's advocate, standing shoulder to shoulder with them, working to fortify the edges of their lives against prejudice and discrimination.

And yet, in one moment of carelessness, I had joined the ranks of those who taunt, tease, and belittle. Like water from a bursting dam, my words spewed out, escaping. Though wishing so, I could not call them back. I did it, and I was so sorry.

I saw the look in my son's eyes as he ran off to his room. I felt heavy with sorrow and sick at heart. Tears began to flow down my cheeks, followed by large gulping sobs. Going into my bedroom, I started to kneel to pray for forgiveness, but as I did, I felt strongly impressed that I needed to ask someone else's forgiveness first.

Going into my son's bedroom, I found him sitting quietly on the edge of his bed. "Hey, buddy," I said, ruffling his hair. "Can I talk to you for a minute? I need to ask you something."

I bent down in front of him so that I could look at him. "I made a terrible mistake," I said, trying to hold back the tears. "I should never have talked to you that way or used those kinds of words. Sometimes, even grown-ups make mistakes."

"Yeah," he said.

"I'm so sorry—so very sorry," I said. "Can you forgive me?"

"Yeah," he said, with a little smile, wrapping his arms around me.

The memory of that day has stayed with me through the years. Now, when I am tempted to speak in anger or use words that belittle, I try to remember the overwhelming feeling of regret and sorrow that engulfed me that day. I take a breath and try to do better.

I also try to follow my son's example of forgiveness. He was so willing to readily embrace me and forgive me. I want to be more like him. When someone hurts my feelings, I try to freely forgive, as he did. Just as our Father does.

— Jeannie Lancaster —

My Prayer

*Dear Father, please help me to remember to pause
and think before I speak. Give me the wisdom to
know when to close my mouth and open my heart.
If I have hurt someone, let me go to him or her
and ask forgiveness. Most importantly, thank you,
Father, for your forgiveness, which changes my life.
Amen.*

74

The Easter Dress

*For you created my inmost being; you knit me together
in my mother's womb. I praise you because
I am fearfully and wonderfully made...*
~Psalm 139:13-14

"Here, let's try on these two dresses," I coaxed.

"But I don't like green, and the other is too scratchy."

We were shopping for an Easter dress and were no closer to finding one that we both agreed upon than when we first began. What happened to the little girl who didn't care what color the dress was as long as it "twirled" when she spun around? And when did she start noticing the fabric of a dress?

Something was going on, and I was not adjusting well. For years, I simply picked out the dress I liked and brought it home. Sure, the last couple of years I began to notice a change, but I thought it was cute that my daughter wanted to help pick out a dress. She always ended up with my choice, but I thought it was because she and I had the same taste. But here we were, searching for her eighth Easter dress, and things were not going as smoothly as in the past.

"What about this one? It looks so pretty on you. We can get a bow for your ponytail."

With downcast eyes, she whispered, "I don't want to wear my hair up. I want to wear it down."

Okay, so I could deal with the hair, but I still wanted the dress. Gently, I said, "We will worry about your hair later. What do you think about the dress?"

She told me it was too frilly, and she didn't like lace. Too frilly... an Easter dress with no frills and lace? I couldn't imagine it. What was next to go? Patent leather shoes?

Before I could take the other dress off the hanger, she held up one I hadn't even seen her bring into the dressing room. Not wanting to cause another scene, I left her alone. I watched her pull the plain beige dress with blue flowers over her head and adjust the front so the dainty buttons were in a straight line. She tilted her head and smiled at her reflection in the mirror.

"Mom, this is the one I want," she announced proudly.

I began to try and talk her out of it when I noticed her eyes glistening with fresh tears. As I looked into her beautiful dark eyes, I heard her softly ask, "Do you not think what I like is pretty?"

Oh, my. I was taken back with the realization that this child before me was not me, but her own person—the person God created her to be. God quickly spoke to the Spirit within me and reminded me that my daughter was woven by Him in my womb.

With tears in my own eyes, I reached out to touch the sleeve of my daughter's dress.

"It's perfect," I said.

Just like my daughter... "fearfully and wonderfully made." Never again would I try and change who God had created her to be.

— Beth K. Fortune —

My Prayer

Dear Lord, help me to see my child as You see her. Help me to be aware that as she grows, she is following the desires that You placed in her and becoming the woman that You intended her to be. Yes, she is wonderfully made, and I thank You for knitting this beautiful child in me.

Amen.

75

Busted

If we claim to be without sin, we deceive
ourselves and the truth is not in us.
~1 John 1:8

"Mommy, is the policeman going to take us all to jail?" Receiving a speeding ticket with all four of my small children watching from the back of the van was not on my to-do list for the day. As I rolled up the window, I watched the policeman in the rearview mirror striding back to his squad car. Of course, we weren't going to jail—it was just a ticket. But my emotional response to the incident was just as over the top as my child's fearful question—and just about as disproportional.

That policeman should have been out catching real criminals—not a carpool mom! I was angrier that I had been caught and given a ticket than I was sorry for speeding. My attitude was wrong, and I knew it.

As I took a deep breath and turned to survey my four children buckled in behind me, I realized that my speeding ticket offered a front-row vantage point for a real-life lesson. Whatever I said next to my wide-eyed young audience would be an unforgettable lesson about life. But would it be the right one?

Youngsters learn more from what they observe in our behavior than from what they hear us say. How could I model anything less? The day I became a mother and peered with awe into the face of my firstborn infant, I felt a heavy responsibility. This child's spiritual life and perception of God would rest mostly on how well I did as a parent.

A perfect parent—that's what I determined to be. However, keeping up that facade would prove to be exhausting, somewhat like cleaning the bathtub while wearing Rollerblades. It was also dishonest, for to be perfect means to be sinless, and the Bible has a stern warning about that: "If we claim to be without sin, we deceive ourselves and the truth is not in us" (1 John 1:8).

My children will grapple with sin their whole lives for they are the offspring of Adam and Eve, as I am. I battle with sin daily, and they will, too. So perhaps a more valuable parenting lesson is not how to be perfect, but what to do when we fail in our struggles with sin.

What did I finally say to my children after the policeman gave me the speeding ticket? "Even Mommy has rules to obey, and sometimes I blow it."

Getting ticketed for breaking the law may not have been my finest parenting moment, but it did provide a golden opportunity to teach my children one of life's essential lessons: We will all sin, and when we admit our wrongs, grace abounds. It is the truth—the gospel truth.

— Rhodema A. Cargill —

My Prayer

Lord, thank you for your grace that abounds when we admit our faults. Help me to be more concerned with being honest and humble before my children than always appearing righteous. Let me be quick to admit my wrongs and ask forgiveness.
Amen.

76

The Tattooed Stranger

*"The King will reply, 'I tell you the truth,
whatever you did for one of the least of
these brothers of mine, you did for me.'"*
~Matthew 25:40

He was scary. He sat on the grass with his cardboard sign, his dog (actually, his dog was adorable), and tattoos running up and down both arms and on his neck. His sign proclaimed him to be hungry and in need of help.

I pulled the van over and contemplated him, tattoos and all, in my rearview mirror. He was youngish, maybe forty. He wore one of those bandannas tied over his head, biker/pirate style. If you looked closely, you could see that he had neatly tucked in his shirt, and his things were in a small, tidy bundle. Nobody was stopping for him.

It was hot outside. I could see in the man's very blue eyes how dejected and worn-out he felt. The sweat was trickling down his face. As I sat with the air-conditioning blowing, a scripture suddenly popped into my head: "...whatever you did for one of the least of these brothers of mine, you did for me" (Matthew 25:40).

I reached down into my purse and extracted a ten-dollar bill. My twelve-year-old son, Nick, knew right away what I was doing. "Can I take it to him, Mom?"

I watched as he rushed over to the man, and with a shy smile, handed it to him. "Good," I thought to myself, "now he will at least have a meal tonight."

When Nick got back into the car, he looked at me with pleading eyes. "Mom, his dog looks so hot, and the man is really nice." I knew we had to do more.

We ran to the nearest store and bought our gifts carefully. "It can't be too heavy," I explained to the children. "He has to be able to carry it around with him." We finally settled on a bag of dog food, a chew-toy shaped like a bone, a water dish, two bottles of water, and snacks for the man.

We rushed back to the spot where we had left him, and there he was, still nobody stopping for him. Shaking, I climbed out of the car, with all four of my children following me, each carrying gifts.

I looked into his eyes and saw tears. How long had it been since someone showed this man kindness? I showed him what we had brought and told him I hoped the items weren't too heavy for him to carry. He stood there, like a child at Christmas, and I felt my small contributions were so inadequate. When I took out the water dish, he snatched it out of my hands as if it were solid gold and confirmed that he had had no way to give his dog water. He gingerly set it down, filled it with the bottled water we brought, and stood up to look directly into my eyes, which filled with tears as he said, "Ma'am, I don't know what to say." He then put both hands on his bandanna-clad head and just started to cry. This man, this "scary" man, was so gentle, so sweet, so humble.

I smiled through my tears and told him I would be praying for him. As we all piled into the van and drove away, he was on his knees, arms around his dog, smiling. I wondered where he would sleep tonight.

Although it seemed as if we had helped him, the man with the tattoos gave us a gift that I will never forget. He showed me that no matter what the outside looks like, each of us is deserving of kindness, compassion, and acceptance. He opened my heart.

— Susan Farr-Fahncke —

My Prayer

Dear Heavenly Father, please help me remember that the world is full of people in need. Help me to open my heart more often and show your love through my actions.
Amen.

Having It All

*So do not fear, for I am with you; do not
be dismayed, for I am your God. I will
strengthen you and help you; I will uphold
you with my righteous right hand.*
~*Isaiah 41:10*

When my daughter, Julie, was a first-grader, I was spinning more plates than a circus juggler. Wife, mom, daughter, granddaughter, corporate travel manager, as well as Sunday school teacher, member of the church choir, and assistant troop leader for the Brownies—you could say I had my hands full. Like many young mothers, I'd eagerly bought into the popular 1980s ideal: "Today's woman can have it all."

It wasn't long before I concluded the principle we embraced was a bunch of baloney. Whoever thought it up clearly never tried to do it all, was a native of the planet Krypton, or had one heck of a lot of help crossing the finish line.

Of course, it was possible that I was busy running around in circles on the day that super powers were passed out to the other moms. One thing was certain: There wasn't enough time in my schedule for everything that was crammed into it. Every trip to the car seemed to begin with "Hurry up, we're late!"

And it was bugging me.

On a particularly chaotic day at work, the phones rang off the hook, and I barely stopped long enough to take a sip of coffee. My lunch hour consisted of wolfing down a peanut butter and jelly sandwich, collecting Julie from school, and bringing her back to the office to do her homework while I dove into the pile on my desk.

When it was time to pack up and leave, I was so exhausted that it was all I could do to turn the key in the ignition and put the car in reverse.

Suddenly, Julie gasped in delight and pointed toward the western skyline.

"Mommy, look!"

The sun had set behind the trees, leaving behind smudges and swirls of violet, lavender, peach, salmon, and gold... sublime, breathtaking, soothing, and energizing. I'd never in my life seen such colors.

"Oh, my!" I exclaimed.

There we sat, mother and daughter, mesmerized by a heavenly canvas.

"God must really love us today," said my little girl.

I was deeply touched by her words.

"Indeed," I murmured, stroking her hair, savoring the rare moment of peace that washed over us both.

Later that evening, it occurred to me that I'd been chasing what I already had: a rich, full life with family, home, friends, a great job, a wonderful church. Who could want more? What I needed was someone to help me make sense of it all and keep me sane. Who better than the Giver of Life, the one true Super Power? After all, He was the one who had blessed me in the first place. Through Him, all things are possible. Through Him come strength and rest.

My grandmother used to say, "It's sometimes hard to see the forest for the trees."

How true. When the trees stepped aside, I got a good look at the forest. And it was beautiful.

— Michelle Close Mills —

My Prayer

Heavenly Father, thank you for giving us more than we could ever hope for. Help us to see beyond the busy-ness of daily life, so we may fully recognize your gifts and be truly thankful.
Amen.

78

Timing Is Everything

A man's wisdom gives him patience...
~Proverbs 19:11

Potty-training my twins, I figured, would be a breeze. After all, I was an experienced mommy. I had two older sons who were both potty-trained before their third birthdays. Well, the second one was only a few weeks away from three, but, still, I was proud of myself for starting the job while he was still two. So, two boys down, only two to go. Piece of cake, right? Wrong!

When my twins turned three in December, they still weren't potty-trained. We'd been trying all year. Stickers, M&Ms, toilet targets, a special potty seat, toilet-training videos and books, threats, pleading, Spiderman underwear, and a potty chair that played music when tinkled in failed to persuade my boys that they were done with diapers. There were a few successes and glimmers of hope along the way, but they were all short-lived. We were getting desperate. The boys would be starting summer camp in early June, and there was a strict rule: no diapers! The pressure was on. We only had a few months to accomplish the task.

So, we escalated our efforts. We tried taking the boys to the potty every half hour, whether they expressed the desire to go or not. We tried the "leave them naked all day" approach. Both of these techniques really limited our family's social activities! We even set children's books in the bathroom so they could sit and "read" until nature took its course. It seemed like they would never be trained. And then, suddenly, they were. Something "clicked," and they just decided on their own that they were ready to use the toilet full-time. And that was that. They had their own timing, and it had nothing to do with all the threats we had made or the stickers we'd doled out or the number of times we'd watched Elmo use the potty on a video.

Timing is everything. That's true with so many things in life. How often do we make demands of God for things that we want… right now! We want our dream job right away. We want more money now. We want our health restored immediately. But our timing isn't always God's timing. Just think how spoiled we'd all be if we could just snap our fingers and God would grant all our wishes in an instant. What would we learn by that? We learn and we grow when the timing is right.

When I learned to let go of the need to control the timing with my twins, the seemingly impossible happened, and they were toilet-trained. There have been many other times in my life when I've achieved similar results. Whenever I've quit pushing and allowed myself to relax, secure in the knowledge that God would provide in His time, I've never been disappointed. The next time you are in need, go to God. And then wait and let Him answer your prayers—with perfect timing.

— Susan M. Heim —

My Prayer

Dear Lord, help me to remember that there is a time and place for everything. When things don't seem to be happening according to my timetable, please remind me that you hold the master schedule. I know that when I let go, your perfect timing will be revealed.
Amen.

79

The Old Piece of Junk

When they came to Marah, they could not
drink its water because it was bitter.
~Exodus 15:23

"Why did Dad give us this piece of junk?" My usually mild-mannered, easy-going ten-year-old son echoed my dismay. The car was old and the size of a Sherman tank. It had that musty smell of decaying leather and upholstery—nothing like the cars we were accustomed to driving. But we needed a car, as my car was irreparable, and I cringed at the idea of a car payment. So a free car was attractive—well, almost.

Ever since my divorce, my ex-husband bought my cars. The first year, he gave me a Cadillac. The next year, I got an Oldsmobile. The year after that, I got a Ford. Each year for five years, they kept going down in value. I quipped to friends that if I stayed divorced long enough, they would see me on a moped.

To get out of the marriage, I didn't take any money. Even though our marriage ended badly, my ex had some sense of decency, so he bought my cars. But this one clearly said he had worked through his guilt, and I would soon be on my own. A moped might have been better.

The old Buick he had just bought me was about a half-block long, with fading burgundy paint, and a padded top that was beginning to crack. I shuddered every time I looked at it.

Billy hung his head every time he had to get into it for me to drop him at school or one of his friends' houses. Being a boy, cars mattered.

One day as we lumbered along in our tank, Bill was doing his usual grumbling. "Mom, this piece of junk stinks, and it looks awful. Nobody has a car like this but us. Why did Daddy give it to us?"

"Billy, I have an idea. Do you remember the story in the Bible when the children of Israel murmured and complained in the wilderness when they came to the bitter water? It wasn't until they changed what they said that God made the water sweet. Let's try it. Let's start thanking God for this car and see what happens."

That's the day we began the ritual of getting in the car, putting our hands on the dashboard, and thanking God that we had transportation, that the car ran, and that it had come to us as a free gift.

A few weeks later, my ex-husband won a new Thunderbird Special Edition in a hole-in-one at the country club. He drove a Lincoln, and his new wife drove a Jeep. He sent the Thunderbird to us.

Bill is thirty-five now, but he still remembers the lesson of thanking God for the "piece of junk" and when life doesn't give us everything we want, to thank God for everything we have.

— Jan Brand —

My Prayer

*Heavenly Father, thank you that you can make
the bitter sweet, and give us what we need
even when it looks impossible. Keep our faith strong
when our journey is uncertain,
trusting that you will see us through.
Amen.*

80

Bunny Showdown

Train a child in the way he should go,
and when he is old he will not turn from it.
~Proverbs 22:6

The six-foot-two, two-hundred-twenty-five-pound linebacker leaned against my kitchen counter. His blue eyes had clouded to a stormy gray. This sixteen-year-old was not happy with his one-hundred-twenty-pound momma who had just said, "No."

Let's rewind thirteen years. The blue eyes have turned that same storm-cloud gray. The jaw is set at the identical angle. But that winter day, I faced a three-year-old firmly entrenched in front of the old cedar chest in my bedroom.

Normally, as I made my bed each morning, my son, Christopher, would play with the stuffed cloth bunny that sat on top of the chest. When I finished my work, he'd pick up the bunny and return it to its home. Then we were free to build with Legos, play dress-up or empty the lower kitchen cabinets.

But for some three-year-old reason that day, when I told him to pick up the bunny, Christopher balked. I asked again in a firm, no-nonsense, this-is-your-mother-talking voice. His response was a determined glare that said, "Not today. Not ever."

He turned to leave the room, but I stopped him and said, "No, we are going to stay right here until you pick up the bunny." I sat down on the floor. The only threat I made was my comfortable position that announced I wasn't going anywhere.

Our showdown at the Bunny Corral lasted for at least twenty minutes. The busy little guy was not having fun standing still. Every time he tried to walk away from his responsibility, I'd say, "You are not going anywhere until you pick up the bunny." Or, "If you pick up the bunny, then we will go play."

I had a thousand things to do that morning, but I'm grateful God impressed upon me that there was nothing more important than teaching my son to respect and obey authority. Finally, his pudgy little hand reached down, picked up the bunny, and set it on the cedar chest. I thanked and hugged him. Both of us were ready to leave the bedroom and dump out the Legos.

I continued to allow him to play with the bunny, but never again had a problem with him refusing to return it to its home.

Later, I thanked God for giving me the stamina to hold my ground against the little rebel. I told my husband: "There are certain battles that we have to fight and win. We can either fight those battles when he's three or when he's sixteen."

Flash forward to the six-foot-two linebacker who is not happy with his mother's current decision. It's not the first time, and I'm sure it won't be the last. But my little rebel is now an Eagle Scout who has developed a respectful attitude and a habit of obedience. Whenever Christopher finds himself in a situation that requires he respect parental authority, school authority, or the authority of the law, he is equipped and protected by those lessons learned in the world of Legos, dressing up, and stuffed bunnies.

— Marla Woolsey —

My Prayer

*Father, please give me the strength I will need today
to stand firm in teaching your principles to my child.
We are so fortunate to be children of God,
loved by a Father who gently disciplines us and
forgives our transgressions.
Amen.*

81

Beyond the Sunset

*...live self-controlled, upright and godly
lives in this present age, while we wait for
the blessed hope—the glorious appearing
of our great God and Savior, Jesus Christ.*
~Titus 2:12-13

M y mother lived every day of her life basking joyously in the
sunlight of God's love. Never was this more comforting than
when my mother learned the final days of life were upon her.
While the reality of this news was painful, nothing could have
been more of a loving gift than the eye-opening experience of watching her close down her life.

From the time her cancer was diagnosed, our mother was given
three months to live. Accepting this sentence as yet "another phase of
my life," as she called it, she went about, in her words, "completing"
things. She began by visiting each of her children, and then friends,
relatives and community members, telling them how much she'd
appreciated and loved them. She asked for forgiveness if she had
wronged them in any way.

Next, Mom went through closets, cabinets and drawers, boxing and distributing certain mementos, photo albums and keepsakes for each of her children and grandchildren. Then, she gathered us children around to help her "tie up loose ends," assigning each one of us things to do, such as helping her select a casket, write her obituary, or locate her favorite hymns and Scripture to be used in the funeral service.

Then came the "photo phase," a ritual in which Mom went around the house looking at the many photos of her family over the years one more time. She would pick up a picture, study it, dust it and either return it to its place or turn it upside down. Seeing her do this, I asked her what it meant. "Oh," she said, referring to the picture she held in her hands of my sister and I when we were small girls in cute, look-alike sundresses, "I just love you all so much. Look, this was taken in Seattle…" And then she proceeded to tell me about this treasured time in her life as a young married woman with small children. With the telling of the memory came tears, and then a decision: She returned it—upright—to the shelf. "I think maybe I'm not so done with this memory," she said.

Taking her in my arms, I asked, "Mom, what is this experience like—the closing down of one's life?"

"Well," she replied, "going home to God is tearful, but not fearful. I am ready to be with my Heavenly Father. Preparing to go Home is what this lifetime is about, so there is a joyful love in that this is what I'm doing now. It's a feeling unlike any love I've experienced, including the love a mother feels for her children or a wife feels for her husband. So it's my obligation now to let go of everything that was a part of this life. Some things are easy. Others are not so easy. But whenever I feel heavy-hearted, I feel God's hand upon my shoulder, comforting me."

One week later, everything in my mother's house had been dusted and lovingly turned over. And on that day, my mother allowed her illness to take her to bed and, shortly thereafter, to carry her beyond the sunset, and into the light of a life she confidently knew to offer more love than this world ever could.

— Bettie B. Youngs —

My Prayer

Dear Father, help me to live every day of my life "right with God." May I be an example to my children in preparing in this lifetime to go "home." When it is my time to take that last breath on Earth, I hope to go with sunshine on my face, knowing that I am firmly in the grasp of your hands.

Amen.

82

Rebuilding Castle Walls

*It is God who arms me with strength
and makes my way perfect.*
~2 Samuel 22:33

K ansas winters are rough, especially when your child's attitude is colder than the raging blizzard outside your door. Weeks of frigid temperatures and bleak forecasts buried our family's endurance as surely as layers of ice, snow, slush, and mud buried our acreage. On top of that, our little country home nestled in the Flint Hills is winter-accessible only via four-wheel-drive vehicles. And ours sat in the shop, awaiting repairs.

We awoke one blustery day to much bigger problems. My older daughter's attitude froze everyone within a two-foot radius. We'd had a mini blow-up the night before, when I told her and her sister to clean their room. They'd launched a new "play idea" and had arranged everything into little rooms of a castle. Problem? It was bedtime, and the room-clog needed to go! Besides, this maze was a middle-of-the-night accident waiting to happen. Unaccustomed to this kind of angry revolt from my children, but chalking it up to cabin fever, I blithely tucked them in and didn't think twice about it.

So, the next morning, as promised, I went in and helped rebuild "the castle" for resumption of their playtime enjoyment. Carry on, troops! Right?

Wrong. All moms can identify with the frustration of having a child who refuses to "snap out of their snit." This emotional teariness was so unlike my eight-year-old. She absolutely would not drop the negativity. She announced she wasn't going to play, and when we ignored her and made the castle bigger and better, her pouting increased.

I've noticed that sometimes parenting seems to be sunshine and blue skies, and then suddenly, some outright rebellion slaps me in the face—kind of like the weather in Kansas. Lemonade one day, hot cocoa the next! It's easy to let the little things slide when, for the most part, my children have been trotting right along being the best kids in the universe!

So I admit to floundering when I finally confronted my eight-year-old about her attitude. I waited till she was alone and reminded her that it wasn't "the worst day in the world." We talked about how we react when really bad things happen, such as losing a loved one. The hardest of times seem to stun our hearts toward God, and acknowledging our great need for Him gives us strength to deal with our crisis and help those around us. How ironic that we tend to "lose it" with the little things or dismiss them as too insignificant to bother God about—like crumbled castle walls. We talked a bit longer; mostly, she aired more complaints.

I left her room, praying to God for a breakthrough, but weighed down by a blizzard of doubts. Had anything I said gotten through? A little later, she came to me. She apologized, asked my forgiveness, and started listing all the things she was thankful for. How hard to admit being wrong—even to your parent. Amazingly, the things she became thankful for were the things she complained about earlier. Only God's grace can complete that kind of turnaround.

Later that day, we unleashed our pent-up emotions with wild abandon. Whooping and whooshing, we conquered the best of our icy slopes on sleds.

Sometimes, parenting seems like guesswork in the face of an angry, hurting child. Preaching at them won't work. The "talk" shouldn't be reaction-spawned or critical. Encourage them with reminders of why God's way is the best way. Maybe share a story of how you learned the hard way. Then leave the room… and pray hard!

— Mary L. Allen —

My Prayer

Lord, thank you for being with me when I'm floundering, for loving me and guiding my words, and for working some parenting miracles in the process.
Amen.

83

God's Glittery Gift

*Just as each of us has one body with
many members, and these members do
not all have the same function, so in
Christ we who are many form one body,
and each member belongs to all the
others. We have different gifts, according
to the grace given us.*
~Romans 12:4-6

"Kayla, Kayla, Kayla," my daughter, Bayley, screamed. "Why
can't you be normal like the rest of us? Why does everything
have to be princess?"

My normally patient older daughter was right. I've never
understood how I managed to end up with my daughter Kayla. At
times, our differences drive me to the edge of sanity. I have no idea
how to relate to a little girl obsessed with princesses. People often ask
me where she gets it. I truly believe it is simply how God made her.

I never imagined that I'd pray about princesses—to ask God to
teach me so I could accept my daughter for who she is. Loving her
has never been the issue. But finding a way to connect with her and

appreciate her for being a princess was a difficult task.

Why did my daughter have such a strong need to be a princess? We had never been pink and frilly sort of people. No one had ever encouraged her to be a girly girl. I knew that was how God made her, but I didn't understand why. Surely a family who liked those things would be a better fit for my little girl. I mourned my inadequacies as a mother who would never be able to teach my daughter the other lessons she'd want to learn—like about girly things.

Shortly after my older daughter's outburst, I reached a breaking point. My younger daughter had absolutely driven me nuts. I sat on my couch, sobbing. "God, why did you give me Kayla? My older daughter, I can handle. But Kayla? I know nothing about raising her. This poor kid is going to be messed up for the rest of her life because I don't know how to be a good mom to a princess. Why, God? Why her?"

Though I hadn't said the prayer out loud, it was as if Kayla had been listening. She came skipping into the room, tossing glitter everywhere. Glitter. I almost started sobbing hysterically because my daughter had ruined the vacuuming I'd just finished.

And then I felt God whisper into my heart. Glitter. Without Kayla, there would be no glitter in your life. Everyone needs a little glitter in their life.

It wasn't about what we could give Kayla, but what Kayla could bring to us.

At that moment, Kayla caught sight of me and realized she was about to get in big trouble for making a mess. I smiled at her, gathered her in my arms, and thanked God for knowing that we didn't need another person just like us. We needed someone who would enhance our lives with her differences, adding glitter to our lives.

— Danica Favorite —

My Prayer

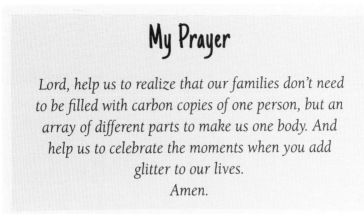

Lord, help us to realize that our families don't need to be filled with carbon copies of one person, but an array of different parts to make us one body. And help us to celebrate the moments when you add glitter to our lives.

Amen.

84

An Instrument in God's Hands

Even a child is known by his actions,
by whether his conduct is pure and right.
~Proverbs 20:11

During my son's first year of piano lessons, I regretted letting him learn to play. He begged me to let him take lessons, but after a while he lost his initial enthusiasm. There were many times when I wanted to say, "All right. That's it! We're stopping." But I didn't. I knew that was just what Joshua wanted to hear.

Up to this time, we had had a good relationship. Now that was being tested. I dragged him to lessons and daily nagged him to practice. Joshua would either ignore my request, make excuses, or argue with me. So why was I putting us through this stress?

Was it always going to be this way? I prayed for wisdom.

Then I suggested that Joshua ask Joe, his teacher, to teach him to play the songs Joshua liked in addition to the pieces in his lesson book. The songs Joshua heard in music class at a Christian school became the key to a turnabout in his attitude and behavior toward me and the piano.

And so began Joshua's journey on the road toward making a joyful noise unto the Lord. Our half-hour lesson each Monday became a blessing. Why didn't I think of this before? I reproved myself. Music lessons were no longer a chore.

Now Joshua brings a "religious favorites book" to his sessions and is learning a new hymn each week. As Joe teaches my son these pieces, God alone knows what impact the words of these sacred songs will have on Joshua and his teacher. At a recent Sunday afternoon recital, Joshua was asked by Joe to play "As the Deer," "Jesus Christ Is Risen Today," and "This Is My Father's World" as part of his repertoire.

Today, Joshua is eleven and in his third year of piano. Playing his chosen instrument gives him a lot of pleasure and us much enjoyment. Above everything else, I'm so thankful that my son has a heart for the Lord and is honoring God through his love of hymns. He, too, is an instrument in God's hands.

— Pat Jeanne Davis —

My Prayer

Dear Lord, you know our child's mind and the intentions of the heart better than we do. Guide us as mothers and help us to be patient so as to prompt our children to Godly behavior and to make right choices. In His name, we ask for this assistance.
Amen.

85

The Seed Planters

For you have been born again, not of
perishable seed, but of imperishable, through
the living and enduring word of God.
~1 Peter 1:23

Spring fever teasers. That's what Mom called the seed catalogs arriving in our mailbox every January. Situated in the cozy sunroom of our home, we'd wistfully pore over page after colorful page of blooming daffodils, tulips, and crocuses. Every once in a while, we'd pause, glancing out the window at the tiny sparrows struggling to find the birdseed scattered beneath the feeders. Shivering, we'd return to our happy pastime, making wish lists and dreaming of the flower gardens we planned on nurturing through the spring and summer months to come.

As I grew older, I discovered those weren't the most important seeds Mom planted with her offspring. Each night before we closed our sleepy eyes, Mom would reach for her Bible. Together, we'd read words of wisdom from the good book.

"Now here's good seed for thought," she'd murmur softly, sharing one of her favorite passages. Her soft voice lulled us into a state of tranquil bliss. There was no place in the entire world we wanted to be at that moment other than lying under the soft, warm quilts listening to Mother's sweet voice sharing God's love letters.

Before I knew it, I was raising children of my own. Like Mom, we wistfully pored over seed catalogs every winter. Our daughters, Autumn and Amber, loved making colorful collages to adorn their bedroom walls. As the sun kissed us goodnight each evening, I'd reach for my Bible just like Mom had, planting the seeds that really mattered.

Our girls are all grown up now and raising families of their own.

Last evening, our older daughter telephoned from Japan where she and her family are stationed in the Air Force. They were just beginning the day.

"Your grandson has something to say to you," Autumn's voice proudly chimed. I could hear three-year-old Everett's little feet pitter-pattering to the phone.

"Good morning, Grandma, I love you! In the beginning, God created the heavens AND the Earth!"

Suddenly, I was transported to the most beautiful flower garden on the face of the Earth.

Mom's seeds were still being harvested.

— Mary Z. Smith —

My Prayer

Father, thank you for giving us your Holy Word.
May those seeds of wisdom be planted deeply within
our hearts so that we will grow to be more like you.
Amen.

86

Footprints

But if we walk in the light, as he is in the light,
we have fellowship with one another.
~I John 1:7

My oldest son, Dave, got married last year. He and his bride, Katie, decided on the date of 09-09-09, loving the quirkiness and the alignment of numbers. Beautiful and quite intimate, the ceremony took place at sunset on a beach in Mexico, and only included the bride and groom, my husband Jeff and me, and Katie's parents, Ken and Debby.

Afterward, the six of us went down to the water's edge, where the photographers were to snap pictures. I breathed deeply of the salt air, relishing the seascape. The horizon stretched out in front of us as far as the eye could see, and the sun, as if stifling a yawn, winked solemnly in its last retiring moments. As we parents stepped back to watch our kids pose for photos, I focused on my son and felt my heart constrict. He'd once been my little boy—mine and mine alone—but now I was in the background. Now I was just "the groom's mom." I sensed a sort of rending, knowing he would never be totally mine again. This was further underscored by his footprints between the tidemarks, impressions in the sand that sat side-by-side with Katie's.

It was oddly that pairing of footprints that gave me comfort.

When Jeff and I first met Ken and Debby, we liked them instantly, but there was one thing that completely endeared them to us when we visited their home. I happened to notice on the sidewalk out front that their children's small footprints had been pressed into the concrete, a permanent reminder of the kids who had once called this place theirs. For many days thereafter, I couldn't get those footprints out of my mind. They said to me that no matter where Katie and her siblings' lives might lead them, they were always going to be anchored right there, back home. It moved me to know that my son would be joining such a special family.

Watching him walk the beach with his new bride on their wedding day, I had the sudden urge to run my fingers through the sand that held his footprints. I loved its granularity, its coarse texture.

Sand is a brilliant thing, but like most of God's geology, we tend to take it for granted. Each granule is unique, yet it's those very granules that can be molded into a composite whole. When sand rubs against our skin, it can be abrasive. It can rub us raw if we let it, but if we mold it in precisely the right way, we can fashion it, sculpt it, and build sand castles. Sure, it shifts and washes away, leaving sediment in its wake, but it is likewise the foundation on top of which our footprints can be laid.

When Dave and Katie finally finished their photos and walked back up the beach, I was startled to note their footprints. There they were, plain as day, shimmering in the sand and leading right back up to us.

— Theresa Sanders —

My Prayer

*It's not easy letting go, dear God, but help me to
remember that footprints don't necessarily lead
"away from," but "back to." Bless my children,
and let them withstand the wash of time,
the roughage of sand, remaining ever malleable.
Mold them as you will, and may their footprints
lead them home to you.*
Amen.

87

My Black-Eyed Susan

Dear children, let us not love with words
or tongue but with actions and in truth.
~1 John 3:18

"Will I ever have a positive relationship with my daughter?" I questioned once again.

"Wait until she's twenty-one," a friend advised. "Everything will change then."

Twenty-one? I wanted to enjoy my daughter now. But as Susan struggled with being a teen, a close relationship seemed impossible. We could not agree on anything, and with Susan fighting relentlessly for her independence, we were arguing about everything. Like the flower, my Black-Eyed Susan had always brightened our home. But in her teen years, Susan's dark eyes flashed daggers that could pierce the soul. What happened to my darling little girl? "Oh, Lord," I pleaded, "I want her back! I don't even think she likes me, and I'm not sure I like her either."

"Loving and liking are not the same, Karen," God would whisper in my heart.

I knew I needed to act loving, regardless of how she responded. I wanted to see her through God's eyes. Each time I faced another confrontation with Susan, I would consciously choose to love. It was easier said than done, but each time I asked God for His love to replace my inadequacy, He gave it. Still, clashes were frequent, making my husband and I realize there needed to be space between us. More than once, either by her choice or ours, Susan found herself living with someone else until she wanted to return home.

A few years passed, and Susan became a senior in high school. Our move to Michigan from Florida at that time wasn't easy for her, but somehow Susan sensed that my despondency over the move was stronger than hers, and I began to feel her empathy. Cracks were showing in my veneer of self-sufficiency, revealing a part of me Susan had not seen before. The love I'd chosen to express toward Susan began to once again be returned. A friendship emerged, and we actually found ourselves looking forward to spending time together.

Adjusting to her new surroundings, Susan began to make new friends—and one in particular became that special someone with whom she would choose to spend the rest of her life.

One afternoon, as plans were being made for the wedding, I was overwhelmed by the thought of her leaving. Susan and I had just begun to enjoy each other's company, making up for lost time. I wasn't ready to give her up to someone else.

As Susan continued to talk about her wedding plans, I attempted to put my thoughts aside and concentrate on what she was saying. I turned back just in time to hear, "Mom, I want you to be my Matron of Honor. You're the best friend I have."

This time, my Black-Eyed Susan's eyes radiated pure love.

— Karen R. Kilby —

My Prayer

Father, as we struggle in our relationships with our children, help us to see them through your eyes. Your love overcomes any obstacles and barriers that may exist between us. Thank you for giving us the ability to show your love by our actions.
Amen.

88

Turtle Talk

...the Spirit helps us in our weakness.
~Romans 8:26

"You should try to answer some questions at school tomorrow," I prodded my shy four-year-old as we drove home from preschool. "I bet your teacher doesn't know what a great reader you are."

Looking up from behind her wire-rimmed glasses, Emily's lips curled into a frown. "It's hard to talk, Mama."

I sighed, remembering the previous day in the carpool pick-up line.

"She's sure a quiet one," the teacher said, reaching out to hoist Emily into her booster seat. "Bet she has a lot to share."

She sure does, I wanted to say. You should hear her read *Goodnight Moon* and *Brown Bear, Brown Bear*! I thought back to Emily's one-year visit to the pediatrician, where she shocked the doctor by parading around the room in her diaper, correctly naming the colors on the striped wallpaper. Though she said "boo" for "blue" and "wellow" for "yellow," there was no hiding her intellect. A self-taught reader, Emily seemed like a good candidate for preschool. But from day one, tears filled my daughter's bright blue eyes at school drop-off time. She withdrew like a turtle, hiding in her shell and not talking to anyone — teachers or fellow students.

"She doesn't want to come with us to music," the teacher said. "She just sits in her chair."

The next day at drop-off time, I shut off the ignition and turned to face my daughter. Sitting in her car seat, holding a tote bag decorated with red handprints, Emily looked up at me expectantly.

"I want you to try to talk a little bit today," I began.

Emily squirmed in her booster seat. "But it's hard, Mama."

"I know it's hard, but when you can't do something on your own, God can help you. He is always with you, even in preschool. When it seems really hard to talk, just ask God for help."

With that bit of advice, Emily was off, whisked out the car door by a teacher's aide. I dreaded the next two hours. Would Emily spend the time sitting alone in a chair, when she should be playing dress-up and kneading play dough with her friends? Why couldn't she act like a "normal" preschooler?

At pick-up time, the teacher rapped on my car door.

Oh, no. Not more bad news.

"What was up with Em today?" The teacher broke into a huge smile. "She was an absolute chatterbox!"

A shiver rose up my spine. "Don't know," I said, smiling as Emily hopped proudly into the car.

But I did know, and Emily did, too. When she needed help the most, God was there, cheering and pulling her from her shell.

Thank you, I prayed as I drove toward home, for helping my little turtle crawl safely from her shell.

— Stefanie Wass —

My Prayer

Dear God, help me to teach my children to turn to you
for strength. Please remind me that you know each
of us by name, and we need only come
to you first with our concerns.
Thank you for your steadfast love.
Amen.

89

The Rocking Chair

As a mother comforts her child,
so will I comfort you.
~Isaiah 66:13

I t sits there vacant and still most of the time now, its upholstery out of vogue for the last twenty years. But I can think of nothing that would prompt me to get rid of it, especially now that a grandchild has been added to the family.

In 1981, I was working for a man who rented out storage units. Often when people were behind on their rent payments, the contents of their units would be seized and disbursed. Most of it was pretty worthless, including a beat-up old rocker my boss offered to me, knowing our first baby was due to arrive in a few months. It was the ugliest thing I'd ever seen. Covered in orange vinyl, every crack and crevice showed dirt and wear. For all I knew, mice had nested inside. But with my husband still a college student, I was in no position to turn up my nose at the gift, so I sat down to "test drive" the chair. It was comfortable! And it rocked. We took it home, and scrubbed it down with a brush and a strong solution of some sort. I spent the next several weeks crocheting an afghan to throw over the chair. By the time the baby arrived, it was ready for him. The chair became the place to feed and comfort my little son while providing wonderful, regular breaks for a weary young mother.

Shortly after the birth of our second child, a daughter, we re-upholstered the chair in a velvet burgundy-almost-chocolate-brown with cream-colored pin dots. The chair was now a proud addition to our living room and no longer needed to hide under an afghan. Our family photo albums have pictures of our two oldest kids sharing the chair while reading a storybook, quarreling and crying in the chair, and all three of us in the chair with their unborn baby brother creating a huge mound in the center. By the time he arrived, the chair had become "the answer." It was my answer for a child who was tired, sick, frightened, or recovering from disciplinary measures. Pull him or her up on my lap, wrap a blanket around us both, and rock. I would rock like mad sometimes, trying to soothe the tears—sometimes theirs, sometimes my own—as desperate pleas for help rose from the chair up to heaven.

Then, one September, three significant events happened in the same week that caused me to look at the chair in a different light. On Tuesday, our older son, then twenty, started classes at a Christian university 1,500 miles from home, all on his own with an empty bank account but a heart full of faith. I ached with pride, fear, joy, worry, love, and anticipation. How I'd have loved to take his six-foot-four frame and pull him into the chair one last time to rock.

On Wednesday, our youngest, at fourteen, started high school. I had to bribe him to win so much as a hug by this time. We'd sometimes fight over the chair, but we never shared it anymore. Had I the strength, I'd wrestle him into my lap and rock him once again.

On Thursday, our daughter, who was eighteen and working as an au pair in Switzerland, called us crying, "I want to come home." She'd had sole charge of the two children she cared for while their parents were away for a week, and she'd contracted a virus. Who doesn't want their mom when they're sick? How I longed to wrap my arms and my blanket around her and once again rock her in the chair. Instead, all we could do was pray for her, and assure her of our love and of God's presence.

So it sits there empty, a symbol of comfort, nurturing, and prayer. But I realize that the chair itself was never truly the answer. It was just a tool to demonstrate love and faith... faith in a God who is the real answer, and who has an enormous rocking chair of his own that no one will ever outgrow.

— Terrie Todd —

My Prayer

Lord, I need your strength to be a good mom today and every day of my children's lives. When I need comforting myself, remind me to come to you first. You are our Heavenly Father and always know just what we need.
Amen.

A Family That Plays Together Stays Together

Two are better than one, because they
have a good return for their work:
If one falls down, his friend can help him up.
But pity the man who falls and has no one to
help him up!...A cord of three strands
is not quickly broken.
~Ecclesiastes 4:9–10, 12

It was one of those days when my children were just bugging each other. The rain had been pouring for hours, they were tired of TV, and they couldn't find a thing to do in the house. "Why don't you try playing with your dolls? Or your Legos?" I said, offering suggestions. But with each of my ideas, the response was a one-syllable "Naw." They were bored, and the best way to combat being bored was to start an argument. Pretty soon, petty fights were sprouting up around the house, much like weeds in my garden. By the end of the afternoon, I felt like a referee in a boxing match. "I want all of you to go to your rooms and chill out for a while," I growled to them. "I have had it with your negativity!"

They all scampered to their rooms, knowing that Mom had reached her limit. I sat on the couch taking a quiet moment for myself. It would do us all good to have a little time alone right now. After about ten minutes or so, I heard the first sound of a giggle. Getting up, I decided to find out what was so funny. I made my way up the hallway and listened outside their doors. It took me a moment before I realized they were playing a version of the telephone game. They were passing secret messages to each other through the walls and laughing about the mixed-up results.

I smiled as I listened to the game continue. Like most siblings, they knew which button to push to get a reaction from each other. Yet, almost like magnets, they couldn't stand being apart for too long. That is the way it is with kids. They can be fighting one minute and the best of friends the next. Seeing that the bickering had passed, I called them out of their rooms. The three of them scampered off with a renewed interest in building a fort out of the assorted blankets, towels, and chairs in the house. And, for now, peace prevailed.

As I made my way back to the living room, I couldn't help but feel so blessed. Had God really given me these three amazing children to raise? And could I do His work? All three are unique and different in their personalities. Yet, the bond of family keeps them together. But what does the future hold for them? Sometimes, it scares me to let them grow up in this confusing and sometimes frightening world. Right now, I can control what goes on in their lives and help them make most of their decisions. But, as they grow older, they are going to seek out other friends and situations that I can't control. What will I do when I am relegated to the sidelines and forced to watch them solve their own problems? How will Mom help then?

I do know that I will pray hard and pray often. I will certainly call on the Lord to send me His wisdom and strength to get us through the years ahead. And then I will have to trust that my children were raised as Christians with good values and morals. And when the times get tough, they turn to the Lord to help them get through it.

God lovingly trusted me to raise these children, and it is a gift that I value each and every day. I am so grateful that God has blessed my children with siblings. As a family, our lives are intricately entwined, but thankfully it is God who holds us all together.

— Karen C. Talcott —

My Prayer

*Dear Lord, thank you so much for our families.
Help us to raise our beloved children with separate
identities, yet always with the understanding
that our cord is stronger when we are together.
Guide our children in their future decisions and help
them to always turn to you for guidance when life gets
complicated.
Amen.*

91

Mama Bird

*Know therefore that the LORD your God
is God; he is the faithful God,
keeping his covenant of love to a thousand
generations of those who love him and
keep his commands.*
~Deuteronomy 7:9

One spring day on my drive to work, I noticed a flock of birds flying above my Jeep. Four small birds fluttered and puttered as they learned to fly, while the mama bird flapped nearby. All of the baby birds, except one, lifted from their sputter to an even glide. That one little bird fought to resist the pull of gravity as he struggled to stay afloat. As I stole upward glances from time to time, I noticed the mama bird soar closer to her stumbling offspring. Finally, with a few wing flutters, the mama steadied herself underneath him. As the baby's altitude dropped, the mama bumped him up gently to help him take to the air. Each time she bumped him, the little bird found more courage to fly.

When I pulled away from the flock, I thought about how much that baby bird trusted his mama. She verified that trust when she lifted him up, ever so gently, and helped him find his wings.

Like baby birds, children depend on their mothers and fathers to care for them, feed them, clothe them, and love them. My daughter recently gave birth to a son, and I love to watch her cuddle her baby boy. When she smiles into his tiny face, his eyes are firmly focused on hers. Instinctively, he trusts her to take care of him.

God wants us to trust in Him for all of our needs and with all of our hearts, especially when it comes to our children. In the book of Deuteronomy, we read that God is faithful to thousands of generations. That includes our babies. Throughout our lives, our children see God and learn to trust Him through our words and actions. As your children grow and spread their wings, be prepared to fly nearby and support them with your love and guidance. Build that support through sharing the Bible and praying with your little ones. It is never too early to introduce them to their Creator. And when it is time for your little birds to fly off on their own, you can feel confident knowing that God will keep them in His sight.

— Penny Frost McGinnis —

My Prayer

Dear Heavenly Father, as a mother I seek your face and your wisdom as I raise my child. I trust in you, and ask that my eyes and heart will be open to your Word and your guidance. Help me to direct my child's path just as you direct mine. Thank you for your faithfulness in my life.
Amen.

92

Growing Up, Not Away

*Only be careful, and watch yourselves
closely so that you do not forget the things
your eyes have seen or let them slip from
your heart as long as you live. Teach them
to your children and to their
children after them.*
~Deuteronomy 4:9

March second will be a special day in our home. It's the day
my daughter graduates from little girl to teenager. Yes, the
exciting-for-her-but-dreaded-by-her-parents thirteenth birthday is arriving.

As her dad and I think back thirteen years, we remember the little
baby all soft and sweet-smelling who cooed for our approval and love,
the toddler we watched learn to walk and talk, and the little girl who
shouted "Watch me!" with each new task mastered. We recall all the
times our child came to us to help fix her boo-boos or have us laugh
at her silly made-up jokes. Now we are entering a whole new phase

of life with a teenager.

This was the age I remember growing away from my mother. I thought she was so out of date. She didn't listen to the coolest music or know the hottest singing group. (Rock and roll was my choice, while she had big band music playing.) She didn't know the hippest dance moves, and her clothes were atrocious. She didn't even own a pair of jeans until she was in her sixties. Her idea of fun was reading the latest bestseller or taking me to the nearest 7-Eleven for a Slurpee and a comic book. Mom wasn't cool, and I wanted to be as far away from her as possible.

As I traveled from cool teen to grown-up mom of a twenty-first-century teen, I have found myself switching places with my mom. It's not fun to suddenly realize that I am now the uncool mom. My music—though it's more up-to-date than my mother's was—is still not twenty-first-century stuff. As far as dancing goes, slow and easy is my style now. Clothes I pick today are for comfort and convenience. I choose straight leg jeans, whereas my daughter wouldn't dream of wearing anything but bellbottoms. For fun, I would rather take a walk with a friend or see a "chick flick," as my husband calls them. Not exactly what my daughter would call a dream evening.

So how will I be different from my mother? For one thing, I don't plan to settle for the generation gap. I can listen to my daughter's music and share with her the great oldies that I loved. I can look at the latest dances and show her my old moves that made me think I was hot stuff. I can't say I will change how I dress, but I can be open to her choices and respect them. Fun for any age can be games, bowling, or skating, as long as we do it together. Hopefully, my daughter and I can bridge the gap in ways that my mother and I never did.

Yes, her thirteenth birthday will be a day to remember—and the beginning of a whole new relationship. I look forward to it a bit timidly, but also with excitement about what the future will bring.

— Patricia Downs —

My Prayer

Help us, Lord, as we enjoy the changes that occur in our lives and in the lives of our children. We need you to guide, protect, and comfort us on this wonderful journey. May we always trust that you hold us and our children in your gentle hands.

Amen.

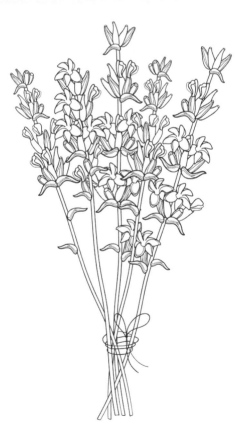

93

The Light Saber vs. the Dandelions

*Therefore do not worry about tomorrow,
for tomorrow will worry about itself. Each
day has enough trouble of its own.*
~Matthew 6:34

B eing a stay-at-home mom can get monotonous at times. The mundane tasks of laundry, cooking, cleaning, and refereeing can make the moments of the day devoid of feeling. One acts more like a robot, tending to the programmed activities for the day, without stopping to notice the surroundings.

On one such day, my youngest son, Luke, begged me to take him to the soccer field across the street from our home. I wasn't in the mood to play soccer, and my robotic tasks had already been programmed. However, it was finally a warm spring day after a very long, cold Michigan winter, so I relented.

He grabbed his purple light saber and headed toward the door. Rewind. Light saber? I thought we were going to the soccer field. Luke wasn't interested in playing soccer after all. What a relief. Then why were we going to the soccer field, and why did the trip involve a light saber? He informed me that he was going to fight battle droids. Okay. I was along for the ride, but I wasn't exactly sure what his intentions were. My son has an active imagination, but even he knows there are no Star Wars battle droid armies awaiting his attack in the local soccer field. How wrong I was!

With the warmer weather came dandelions, the kind that look like cotton balls that can be blown to spread more weeds. In Luke's imagination, the dandelions were now battle droids, and there was truly a large field awaiting his attack. Luke wielded his saber with great skill. I was informed that I was only a Jedi-in-training, having not yet achieved the status of Jedi Master, as he and his older brother Connor had. I could see why, as Luke deftly defeated the battle droid army in the soccer field (i.e., knocked apart the dandelions).

As Luke defeated his armies for the Jedi Alliance, I picked up helicopter seeds that had fallen from the many maple trees growing around the field. Luke took a break to marvel at how the seeds moved like helicopter blades in the sky. For twenty minutes on that early spring day, my son fought the good fight. And I won my battle, too, by breaking away from the household tasks that had been programmed for me the night before.

I realized that I didn't become a mom to cook and clean. No, I became a mom so that I could watch my son fight battle droids in the local soccer field. I became a stay-at-home mom so that I would not miss the moments that happen spontaneously in the life of a child. I still miss a lot when I am home and worrying about the things that I think need to be done. But this time, I was there to watch the Jedi Alliance overcome the enemy. I wouldn't trade that moment for the world.

— Marcy A. Blesy —

My Prayer

God, please help me to see life through the innocent eyes of my child. Help me to appreciate what is right in front of me and stop worrying about all of the things I could be doing.
Amen.

94

The Golden Summer

*You let men ride over our heads; we went
through fire and water, but you brought
us to a place of abundance.*
~Psalm 66:12

We lived far below the poverty level, and yet my kids and I luxuriated in the richness of the countryside where we lived. Millions of tiny peepers gave free concerts outside our windows. Beavers added to the rustic music, slapping flat tails against the swampy lake as they worked. Golden eagles and great blue herons soared above. My daughter Sarah coaxed a white swan to eat from her hand that spring.

In spite of my bad marriage, there was much to be thankful for. Riches crammed every lovely nook of our home place. Goldenrod spilled sunshine around like showers of golden treasure. Bejeweled spider webs hovered between blades of grass, heavy with morning dew. Fireflies painted tantalizing patterns against the black velvet darkness, drifting low to the earth to tempt barefooted children with mason jars.

When my husband abandoned us, we were forced to leave our home and rent an apartment in a nearby small town. My grief was unbearable. Not only had I lost the simple dream of raising my children in peace and beauty, but I knew I could never become the father they needed. Since

I had to go back to work to support us, I couldn't even be the mother I wanted to be. I thought their childhood was ruined.

I wallowed in self-pity for a while, but one day God showed me a better way. While I couldn't give my kids a good earthly father, I saw that God had promised to be the Father of fatherless children. I asked Him that day to give my children everything that I could not and all that their father would not. I believe the beginning of God's answer to this prayer was "the golden summer," as my kids later named it.

To my children, the summer we moved was one long, happy picnic. For the first time in their lives, they had other kids to play with. Organizing a troop of a dozen or so, they fought "apple wars," a game they invented that involved pelting each other with hard green apples from the overgrown tree in the backyard. This had the added benefit of leaving impressive bruises to show off afterward.

Impromptu wrestling matches flared up in the grass in which my daughter often triumphed over the boys. After a brief summer flood, a neighborhood water-football game sprang up in our yard. One steamy afternoon, a friend's father taught Luke the covert art of hand-fishing in the creek. Evenings were spent practicing marksmanship on our neighbor's unfortunate barn, decorating it with fluorescent pink paintball splats.

The bookmobile trundled into town every other Saturday carrying friendly traveling librarians who offered delicious books to be devoured on rainy days. Secrets were whispered as young companions stargazed from the shelter of the tree house. The Fourth of July arrived, and we trooped toward the park, hauling blankets for spreading on the grass. The fireworks were especially fine that year, improved further by the rare treats of cotton candy and freshly pulled taffy.

These are the things my children remember about "the golden summer," not the things they lost. In their minds, its greatness will never be equaled.

Sometimes, I forget that God answers prayers in His own creative way, and rarely in a manner that I expect. My children played carefree that summer, forgetting the unpleasant parts of life with their earthly father. They were safe and cared for then, as they are now. A mother needn't worry when God puts His hand to the task of fathering.

— Rhonda Brunea —

My Prayer

Dear God, what a rich and wonderful world we are blessed to live in! Thank you for being our Creator and our Heavenly Father, who is the perfect parent for our children.
Amen.

95

Picture Perfect

*"Therefore I tell you, do not worry about
your life, what you will eat or drink; or about
your body, what you will wear. Is not life
more important than food, and the body more
important than clothes?"*
~Matthew 6:25

"Someday, this will be funny." That was my thought as I fumed, looking at my daughter, Mindy, in her ratty pink sweatshirt. I told myself not to make a big deal out of it, to quit being so superficial and prideful. But I was still ticked.

We were getting ready for a family photo for our church directory, and I was quite proud of my little ensemble. I had carefully selected color-coordinated clothes for the five of us—my husband, myself, our two sons, and the aforementioned nonconformist. In varying combinations of red, black, and white, my little clan would be fit for the cover of any parenting magazine. I could just envision this perfect photo on our next Christmas card and the admiration from those who saw how together we were. Totally with it!

I never guessed that Mindy, who detested the itchy black sweater with the tiny red pin dots, had left it behind and was wearing instead her beloved pink sweatshirt hidden from my view under a winter coat. By the time this was revealed at the church, there was no time to return home before our scheduled appointment. I knew that if put to a vote, no one would side with me on the idea of rescheduling. I was the only one who cared.

I'm not sure what bugged me more—the open defiance on Mindy's part or the chagrin that I felt as we posed before the camera, squeezing out forced grins. No matter how much I told myself to chill out and not be one of "those" kind of mothers, my disappointment showed, and the kids all knew it. When the photos came back, I rolled my eyes. As an exercise in humility, I went ahead and had it made into Christmas cards and sent them out. Someday, I hoped, Mindy would see what I saw in the picture, and we would laugh.

That day has come. She's now in her twenties, and the photo recently showed up in an anniversary collection.

"That sweatshirt really did look dumb, didn't it?" she chuckled.

Truth is, it looks no dumber than my huge eyeglasses and hairstyle. The photo would be funny now regardless of whether the whole family had complied. But it would never have had the memorable story behind it of a strong-willed little girl and a controlling, proud woman who have since grown to be friends. A subsequent family portrait, taken some seven years later, sits on a table in our living room. It shows the same five people all in their favorite sweatshirts—strangely enough, color-coordinated—and looking thoroughly comfortable and happy just to be together. I guess Mom learned a thing or two about what she can and cannot control.

When things don't go as I planned, I try to remember that family photo. If it's going to be funny someday, why not today?

— Terrie Todd —

My Prayer

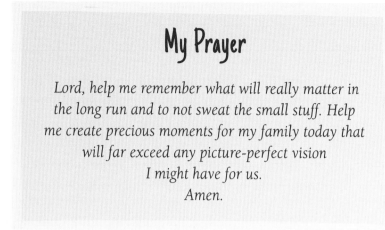

Lord, help me remember what will really matter in the long run and to not sweat the small stuff. Help me create precious moments for my family today that will far exceed any picture-perfect vision I might have for us.
Amen.

96

Mommy's Hero

*And we urge you, brothers, warn those
who are idle, encourage the timid, help
the weak, be patient with everyone. Make
sure that nobody pays back wrong for
wrong, but always try to be kind to each
other and to everyone else.*
~*1 Thessalonians 5:14-15*

As a toddler, my son was adorable, bounding after me with rosy cheeks and blond curls. How could I tell him "no" when he chose to spend all day "helping Mommy" with her chores?

Gardening was Danny's favorite. Being all boy, he loved playing in the dirt. I'd plant seeds, and he'd dig them up. I'd dig a hole, and he'd fill it in. We had "fun" like that all summer, while I tried desperately to plant gardens around our newly built home.

That autumn, I bought dozens of tulip bulbs to bring color to a large, empty garden under my son's bedroom window. But if they were to survive long enough to bloom, I'd have to plant them while Danny was napping. That meant I'd need someone to stay inside with our sleeping toddler. For weeks, I waited for my husband to be available.

Finally, in early December, John was home studying for final exams, so I crept outside during Danny's nap to plant nearly a hundred tulip bulbs. While I worked, snow started falling, slowing my progress considerably, but only a couple of inches fell. Since we lived in Montana, it could have been much worse. Once I'd completed the task, I felt like an Olympian, a genius, and a master of stealth all wrapped into one super-mom!

The next spring, I was delighted to see a colorful mass of tulips burst from the ground under my son's window. What brightness it brought, lifting my spirits after a long winter.

One sunny afternoon, I went from flower to flower, enjoying the beauty, while Danny beat on our chain-link fence with his favorite stick. When he saw me admiring the flowers, he dropped his stick and ran to join me. Embracing a large yellow tulip in his chubby hands, he stuck his whole face inside to have a sniff.

Then Danny jumped back, obviously startled. Pointing to the flower, he whispered, "It got a 'pider, Mommy."

I laughed when I looked inside. The interior parts of the tulip were black. They did look a bit like a huge spider. However, I carefully explained to my toddler that the flowers weren't dangerous. I even put my hand in a few of them to show him they were safe. But Danny just kept backing away in fear.

The phone rang, so I went inside to get the call. A few minutes later, I called Danny in for his nap. After removing his encrusted dirt, I tucked him in bed and went to close the shade on his window.

To my horror, every tulip had been whacked off and beaten into the ground. Danny's favorite stick lay in the grass nearby.

Thankfully, I'd just become a Christian. God subdued the scream welling up inside me. So, instead of erupting in unbridled rage, I paused to take a deep breath, went over to my son, and calmly asked, "Danny... what happened to Mommy's flowers?"

A cherubic face smiled up at me as my son announced, "I killed all the 'piders for you, Mommy."

Though my toddler's grown and gone from home now, he's still my greatest hero.

— Laura L. Bradford —

My Prayer

Thank you, Lord, for restraining my anger on days when I am challenged as a parent. And help my children to reflect the same patience you give to me. May I see the bright side of each difficult moment. Amen.

97

Memories
Set in Stone

*Joshua set up the twelve stones that had been
in the middle of the Jordan at the spot where
the priests who carried the ark of the
covenant had stood. And
they are there to this day.*
~Joshua 4:9

Traditions are an important part of every family—the repetitive things that are a part of the fabric of memories that binds us together. Coming from a household whose only traditions were drunkenness and abuse, I was determined to do things differently when I became a mother. I would give my children something I didn't have: traditions of love.

Our most enduring tradition was completely unplanned. It started with a yellow piece of paper—a recipe in beautiful script handed down to me by my mother-in-law. It was the recipe she used for many years to make my husband's birthday cakes. This lovingly preserved page gave directions for a homemade, four-layer red velvet cake, one with a unique cooked icing, which was different from the traditional southern cream cheese version.

I kept the memories alive that his mother had started by baking the red velvet cake every January for my husband's birthday. Meanwhile, my young children excitedly chose favorite character or cookie cakes as part of their birthday planning. But, one by one, around adolescence, each of our four children began to ask for the red velvet. Before I knew it, this mom was in the kitchen cooking five red velvet cakes every year. And so a tradition passed to another generation.

As my children have grown, some with households of their own, it is still the lure of red velvet cake that gathers us all together on birthdays. We laugh about who gets the biggest pieces and what funny things have happened in the past with the candles. Around one recipe, an amazing number of warm, loving memories have formed.

It now seems that this ritual will continue with a third generation. My six-year-old grandson asked for his first red velvet cake this year. So, on his next birthday, I will take that same yellow piece of paper, now tattered and worn, and bake the cake that will bind three generations together in love.

More than likely, your family has traditions, the moments that bind you together. If you don't, start one. If you can't think of one, borrow one. My recipe is available. Better yet, choose one of your own, or look for one that just happens to find you.

— Deborah L. Kaufman —

My Prayer

Father, let me capture the moments that will endure in my children's and grandchildren's memories. Give me the wisdom to discover and create those traditions that will bind my family together.
Amen.

98

Magical Mirth

A cheerful heart is good medicine...
~Proverbs 17:22

It was a rainy evening in December. School was out for the holidays, and after a long day of shopping, my six-year-old daughter was wound tighter than a top.

Seeking solitude from her silliness, I put on a pot of coffee and retired to the den. All was quiet as I collapsed on the sofa in front of a smoldering fire.

Just as drowsiness set in, I was startled by a burst of laughter coming from Leslie's room. Quite frankly, I was annoyed at being disturbed so soon, and I prayed she didn't venture anywhere near me.

But, alas, within minutes, the laughter floated up the hall toward my haven of rest.

Cracking open one eye, I saw Leslie in the doorway, looking like a missile at countdown. An old walking cane was in her left hand, a poncho swallowed her tiny body, and a pair of sunglasses rested low on the bridge of her nose.

With her eyes glued to mine, she hobbled to the fireplace, plopped down on the hearth, and stared. I had no clue who she was pretending to be, and I had no desire to find out.

After several minutes of silent staring, I felt an uncontrollable case of the sillies come over me as well. Sitting up on the couch, I held out my hand for the cane, which she relinquished without a blink.

Trying not to smile, I pointed it in her direction and announced my intention of casting a spell. True, I didn't believe in spells, but it was a nice thought for one exhausted mother. "This spell," I said, in a very serious tone, "will make you fall on the floor and take a nap."

Leslie didn't crack a smile as I recited a hocus-pocus phrase, moving the cane in small circles, mere inches from her nose. At the end of my magical gibberish, I hollered, "FALL!" hoping she would do exactly that.

Just as the word left my lips, a log in the fireplace crashed to the bottom of the grate with a mammoth boom. After shrieking in terror, my silly girl and I fell to the floor and laughed until we cried.

A nap didn't follow as I had initially hoped, but it no longer mattered. The laughter had produced a little magic of its own. No more stress. No more frayed nerves. No hocus-pocus required.

— Gayle Allen Cox —

My Prayer

Dear Father, at times, the child you gave me to raise eradicates my good cheer. But in one magical moment, she brings it all back again, and I feel restored. Thank you for those moments in our lives that we can cherish forever.
Amen.

99

Love in a Care Package

No, in all these things we are more than
conquerors through him who loved us.
~Romans 8:37

I spotted them as I made my way across campus: a mother robin encouraging her babies to fly. I couldn't help smiling. The babies reminded me of the children I'd been reaching out to during the days I volunteered teaching English as a second language at a local elementary school. It hadn't been too long ago that I was one of those shy little girls being encouraged by my own mom. She continued to show her support while I was in college, sending care packages of love my way just when I needed a hug most.

I missed Mom. She'd worked so hard the past year to finish up her degree at Baptist Theological Seminary in Richmond, and she'd accomplished the task! How could I begin to show her how proud I was of her?

One of the baby robins suddenly spread its tiny wings, flying to a nearby tree branch. I felt like applauding. That baby bird gave me an idea. I'd send my mom a care package brimming with "applause."

I couldn't wait to shop for the care package items. They wouldn't be anything expensive, mind you. Living on a college student's tight budget didn't allow much extravagance. But it was Mom… She'd understand.

That evening, I spread the items I'd purchased on the kitchen table:

A bar of Mom's favorite gardenia-scented soap, thanking her for all the years I'd found freshly scented folded laundry in my dresser drawers.

A dozen chocolate-chip cookies, in honor of all those warm cookies we'd eaten along with tall glasses of chilled foamy milk.

A paperback by her favorite author, reminding me of all the bedtime stories Mom had read to my sister and me before we closed our heavy eyelids for the night.

A bookmark with Mom's favorite scripture, Romans 8:37, letting her know I hadn't forgotten the Godly words of wisdom she had instilled in each of us.

I topped the treasures off with Mom's favorite shade of purple tissue paper, adding a contented sigh.

I couldn't help beaming like the overhead light. It was a beautiful care package for a beautiful woman.

"Thanks, Mom!"

— Emily Collins as told to Mary Z. Smith —

My Prayer

Dear Lord, please constantly remind me to appreciate the important people in my life. Help me show them with my words and actions that they are indeed a blessing from you.
Amen.

100

Laundry Days

Rejoice in the Lord always.
I will say it again: Rejoice!
~Philippians 4:4

With seven kids, I do at least two loads of laundry every night, sometimes more depending on how dirty my husband got at work and how dirty the boys got at play. The dark load goes in after all of the kids have bathed and showered so that by the time there's enough hot water, that load is finished and ready for the dryer. My husband and I then jump in the shower, and when we're done, there's just enough hot water left to wash the light load. Typically by then, the dark load is dry and needs folding. The light load will get put in the dryer before we fall asleep or early in the morning as we all rise and start our day. Two loads a day equal fourteen loads a week. That's a lot of laundry!

When I've had a particularly exhausting day, the last thing I want to do is laundry. As I sort through the dirty clothes, I wonder why the boys can't seem to pull their socks apart instead of leaving them in balls, why the girls can't pull their underwear out of their shorts or pants, and why they all can't seem to sort darks from lights. "Why me?" I ask myself. "I didn't sign up for non-stop sorting, washing, drying, and folding!"

This is the time when I'm gently reminded that I did sign up for this. I did pray for this, and He answered. I did want more children, I did want a husband, and the laundry is just a small part of the bigger picture. God reminds me that my own laundry basket is overflowing with self-pity and bitterness when it needs to be overflowing with gratitude that the kids have clothes to wear and don't have a need for anything. We've been abundantly blessed in so many ways that fourteen loads is a small "price" to pay for what we've been given. As the clothes go through the heavy cycle, so does my attitude. All the stresses of the workday—running children around, dinner on the go, housework, church activities, etc.—get wrung out of me as well.

At the end of each day, I take care of the laundry—and God takes care of me. It might be just allowing me to shed tears for no reason or a gentle reminder that I'm missing out on His purpose for me by focusing on something so inconsequential as laundry. He's definitely cleansed my heart more than fourteen times a week.

— Ami Tripp —

My Prayer

Father, help me to enjoy all parts of my life, even those that seem challenging or monotonous. Continue to wash away my frustrations and renew in me a cleansed heart and soul. It is only through You that we are truly clean.
Amen.

101

Jesus Loves Mommies

Indeed, he who watches over Israel will
neither slumber nor sleep.
~Psalm 121:4

I was utterly exhausted. Our toddler, Jackson, had been waking up in the middle of the night for weeks, and my system was totally out of whack. When we tried to let Jax "cry it out," even for just two minutes, he got so upset that he actually threw up. Talk about frustrating! I tried putting music in his room, giving him a teddy bear, even sleeping with him, but nothing seemed to work.

Whatever the reasons, he got into the habit of "night-waking." He wasn't my first child, but I was at the end of my rope. There wasn't even a pinhole of light at the end of my tunnel. I didn't know what to do.

Then one night during that period of time, as I was rocking the little guy to sleep, I inserted his name into "Jesus Loves the Little Children." I sang, "Jesus loves the little Jacksons, all the Jacksons of the world." I had done the same thing with my now-seven-year-old. Like all children, they loved hearing their names.

On this particular evening, Jackson began asking me to insert other names into the song, like his cousin Molly and his brother Jordan. And then he asked me to put my name in the song. Of course, to him my name is "Mommy." So, to please him, I sang, "Jesus loves the little mommies, all the mommies of the world...."

And I began to think, That's right! Jesus loves all the mommies, even cranky, sleepless moms like me. I smiled as I remembered that in my fatigue and discouragement, Jesus loved me the same as He always had—and He hadn't gone anywhere.

I continued singing, and I thought of all the moms across the world rocking their babies and singing to them at that very moment. I realized once again what a privilege it was to be in the mommyhood, even when it meant getting up at all hours. (At least I knew there were mommies in other time zones that were awake when I was!)

Looking at my baby, I felt a new kinship with my heavenly Father as He reminded me of Zephaniah 3:17: "'The LORD your God is with you, he is mighty to save. He will take great delight in you, he will quiet you with his love, he will rejoice over you with singing.'"

What an awesome thought! He was with me. He wouldn't let me drown in a sea of insomnia and frustration. He saw the thankless job I was doing—and even took delight in it.

My dear fellow moms, did you hear that? He delights in us. He sees every sleepless night, every feverish brow washed, and every puke-y sheet changed. He knows how we love our children and pour ourselves out for them, because He loves us even more—and He, in the form of Jesus, poured Himself out for us on the cross.

As I sang, "Jesus is the Shepherd true, and He'll always stand by you," and put my child to bed (at least for a few hours!), a final thought crossed my mind: Just like moms, God is always "on call."

Now that's a comforting thought!

— Dena Dyer —

My Prayer

Thank you, Jesus, for loving mommies. Thank you
for your love that surrounds us when we are scared,
your grace that covers us when we make mistakes,
and your strength that sustains us
when we are weak.
Amen.

Meet Our Contributors

Gigi Adam has been a farmwife for fifty wonderful years. She and her husband have three sons, along with their wives and thirteen grandchildren. Gigi is very involved in Bible class, and 4-H and Future Farmer livestock projects.

Mary L. Allen lives in the Midwest amidst border collies, horses, a horde of chickens, her husband of seventeen years, and their three girls. When she's not juggling her organic egg business or teaching school, she freelances for several online publications, including her own website, Home-Steeped Hope. Please e-mail her at Mary@homesteepedhope.com.

Linda Apple is the author of *Inspire! Writing from the Soul* and *Connect! A Simple Guide to Public Speaking for Writers*. Her stories have appeared in numerous *Chicken Soup for the Soul* books. Linda is also an inspirational and motivational speaker. Please visit her website at www.lindacapple.com.

Karen Asire has a bachelor's degree in piano pedagogy and a master's degree in counseling. In addition to teaching piano, Karen has published several inspirational articles as well as a book, *Acquainted with Grief*. She resides in South Carolina with her husband and three children.

Lorie Bibbee is a happily married mother of four. She loves sharing God's word and His daily miracles through storytelling, writing, and speaking at conferences. She hopes to continue writing and inspiring others as the Lord allows (and she hopes He allows it a lot!). She prays He encourages you through the words of this book.

A retired high school principal, **Rita Billbe** owns Angels Retreat guesthouse and campground on the White River. Her passions are fly fishing and her church choir. Her blog is www.flyfishing4faith.com.

Shannon Blair's writing passion began with her senior thesis at the University of South Carolina Honors College. Since then, she has been published locally, nationally, and internationally. She teaches two-year college English, and is at work on her first cookbook and a young adult novel series. Learn more at www.shannonblair.com.

Marcy A. Blesy received her bachelor's degree from Millikin University and master's degree from Northern Illinois University. She taught elementary school for seven years before pausing to stay home with her children. Now, with the kids in school full-time, she freelance writes and volunteers in their school. She is editing her first young adult novel.

Laura L. Bradford enjoys encouraging others with stories about faith and family. Her works have appeared in ten anthologies, including two other *Chicken Soup for the Soul* books. She won Grand Prize for her contribution to *A Cup of Comfort for Families Touched by Alzheimer's*.

Jan Brand is a freelance writer who lives in Arlington, TX. She is the Assistant Director of North Texas Christian Writers, and her goal is to see God honored in America again. When asked why she writes, her reply is, "To change the world, one heart at a time."

Rhonda Brunea is a mom and writer living happily in her little miracle home in the country. She is kept company by her two youngest kids, a bunch of dogs, cats and birds, and two sheep who never fail to entertain.

Debbie Cannizzaro received her BA in Elementary Education from the University of New Orleans. She is the author and illustrator of *We Live in Mandeville*. When Debbie isn't reading and writing, she enjoys making wheel-thrown pottery in her home studio. She and her husband Sal have three children: Nicole, Louis, and Joseph.

Rhodema Cargill, a freelance writer and speaker, lives in East Texas with her family. She enjoys speaking to women's groups and Mothers of Preschoolers (MOPS). Her articles have appeared in *Focus on the Family* and *Birds & Blooms* magazines. You can read her blog at www.HerdingWorms.blogspot.com or visit www.RhodemaCargill.com.

Leah Clancy has worked in youth, missions, and women's ministries for fifteen years. She is a native Texan, mother of four, and loves being a pastor's wife. Her interests include writing, scrapbooking, saving money, and living simply. Her other devotions for moms and contact information can be found at www.21piecesofbrave.blogspot.com.

Marie Cleveland is a graduate of Northern State University in Aberdeen, South Dakota, where she currently lives with her family. In addition to being a full-time homemaker, she is the author of two children's books, and also writes poetry and devotionals. Please contact her through her website: www.freewebs.com/mclevelandbooks.

Phyllis Cochran has been published in numerous local and national magazines, *Chicken Soup for the Girlfriend's Soul*, and has published a book, *Shades of Light: A Mother and Daughter's Pathway to God*. She and husband Phil live in Massachusetts and have two children, five grandchildren, and two great-grandchildren. E-mail Phyllis at pacwriter@verizon.net.

Emily Collins of Richmond, VA, attends James Madison University majoring in Interdisciplinary Liberal Studies with a minor in Elementary Education. Emily plans on obtaining her Master's in Teaching and becoming an elementary teacher. She would love to teach English in a foreign country one day. Emily enjoys reading and dancing.

Clara Cooper enjoys sewing, crafts, reading, and travelling. She especially loves teaching children all about the world that God has created around them. Her life's motto is, "The glory of God is the human person fully alive."

Sharron Cosby received her BA from Judson College and BS from Samford University. Sharron enjoys writing, public speaking, and spending time with family, particularly her four grandsons. Her current project is a memoir of her family's struggle with addiction issues. Please e-mail her at prvb3111@aol.com.

Gayle Allen Cox is an award-winning freelance writer from Spring, TX. Her byline appeared in *Chicken Soup for the Soul: Twins and More*, and has appeared in *The Dallas Morning News*, the *Fort Worth Star-Telegram*, and in various other newspapers and magazines. E-mail her at gaylecox@charter.net.

Renee Crosby is an author and speaker with a first book titled *Soup Kitchen for the Soul*. Renee is founder and president of non-profit,

Christian Pep Rally, Inc., which is committed to reviving Christian spirit. Renee enjoys cooking and playing outside with the family. Please contact Renee via her website at www.Christianpeprally.org.

Brendalyn Crudup has been writing poetry and devotionals for several years, and has been published in several book compilations. She is currently writing a series of children's stories for her grandchildren.

Michele Cushatt writes articles, stories, and devotionals from a vast and diverse collection of life experiences. She is the director of a local writers' group, a speaker trainer, and the mother of three teenage boys who tirelessly endure being the subject of her material. Connect with her via her website at www.MicheleCushatt.com.

Pat Davis lives in Pennsylvania with her husband and sons. Her articles, essays, and short stories have appeared in *Chicken Soup for the Soul*, *Guideposts*, *GRIT Magazine*, *The Lookout*, *God Answers Prayers*, *Blessings for Mothers*, and many other publications. She has also written an inspirational romance set in the WWII era. Visit her at www.patjeannedavis.com.

Mary Delgado is a full-time student and mother of two. In addition to writing, she enjoys cooking, reading, hiking, and drawing. She is currently working on her first novel, inspired by the true story of her husband's migration to the United States.

Lola Di Giulio De Maci is a contributor to several *Chicken Soup for the Soul* books. She gathers inspiration for her children's stories from her now-grown children and the many students she's taught over the years. Lola has an MA in Education and English and continues writing from her loft overlooking the San Bernardino Mountains. E-mail her at LDeMaci@aol.com.

Susanne Dietze believes God can put anything to good use, even her overactive imagination. An award-winning author of Christian historical romances, she prays that her words entertain and encourage readers. She's grateful for her family's encouragement and the loving support of her husband and two kids.

Patricia Downs lives in North Carolina with her husband and two teens. In her previous life, she wrote training manuals for a progressive finance company. Today, she enjoys writing about her family, God, and the world around her. She is currently working on a teenage romance novel and several children's books. E-mail her at pedowns@gmail.com.

As a busy wife, mom, and entertainer, **Dena Dyer** constantly loses her keys—but she's holding onto her sanity (barely). Her favorite form of therapy? Writing books to encourage fellow women and mommies. Dena also loves speaking to women's and writers' groups. For more information, visit www.denadyer.com.

Shawnelle Eliasen and husband Lonny raise their five boys in an old Victorian on the Mississippi River. Her work has been published in *Guideposts, Angels on Earth, Marriage Partnership, MomSense, Hearts at Home,* OurPrayer.org, and several anthologies, including *Chicken Soup for the Soul, Christmas Miracles,* and *Praying from the Heart.*

Susan Farr-Fahncke is the founder of 2TheHeart.com, where you can find more of her writing and sign up for an online writing workshop! She is also the founder of the volunteer group, Angels2TheHeart, the author of *Angel's Legacy,* and contributor to more than sixty books, including many in the *Chicken Soup for the Soul* series. Visit her at www.2TheHeart.com.

With four active kids, a husband, and an insane dog, **Danica Favorite** is never short on inspiration for her latest story. She and her family make their home in Denver, CO, where they enjoy the mountain lifestyle with the comforts of the city. You can find her at www.danicafavorite.com.

Beth Fortune served for more than fifteen years in different capacities of the ministry alongside her husband. She now uses her experiences to teach, lead, and encourage others in their walk with the Lord. She is a freelance writer. She and her husband have a daughter in college, three married children, and five grandchildren.

Meagan Greene Friberg is completing her BA degree after taking a thirty-year detour to raise her children. She cherishes time with her husband, their children, grandchildren, and two big, happy dogs. She enjoys writing short stories, camping, church activities, and long lunches with friends. E-mail her at mgreenefriberg@aol.com.

Jenny R. George lives on a five-acre hobby farm north of Coeur d'Alene, ID, with her husband and two children. In addition to publishing more short stories and devotionals, she hopes to publish two books currently in development. For more information about her writing, visit Jenny's website at www.jennyrgeorge.com.

Janice M. Gibson is a mother, teacher, and freelance writer in Aurora, CO. She has taught elementary school for twenty-one years. She enjoys reading, writing, camping, hiking, and church activities.

Kathie Harrington holds a master's degree in speech pathology from Truman State University. She has a private practice, Good Speech, Inc., in Las Vegas, NV. Kathie is a seasoned author, and this is her second contribution to *Chicken Soup for the Soul*. Contact her at www. kathiesworld.com or kathieh2@cox.net.

Carol Hatcher lives in Buford, GA, with her husband Alan and their three children: Colin, Faith, and Grace. This southern mama keeps busy writing devotions for several websites, including her own, www.sheeptotheright.com. Her passion is encouraging others to live out Matthew 25:40 by being Jesus to the people next door.

Robbie Iobst is the proud mom of Noah and happy wife of John. She lives in Centennial, CO, where she is a writer and speaker. If you'd like to get a free "Joyvotion" devotional in your e-mail inbox each week, let Robbie know at robbieiobst@hotmail.com.

Deborah Kaufman has enjoyed working in international adoption and domestic foster care, and teaching English to middle and high school students. She is a wife, mother, and proud grandmother. Deborah enjoys reading to excess, teaching Bible study, and writing inspirational and romantic suspense. You may e-mail her at dlkaufman@bellsouth.net.

Karen Kilby lives in Kingwood, TX, with husband David. She is a Certified Personality Trainer with CLASServices, Inc., as well as a speaker for Stonecroft Ministries. Karen enjoys sharing her life experiences and has had several stories published in *Chicken Soup for the Soul* books, as well as other publications. Contact her at krkilby@kingwoodcable.net.

Karen Krokroskia lives in Kansas with her husband of forty-seven years, Gary. They are both former educators. They have two children and six grandchildren. When not spending time with family and friends, Karen is busy preparing a weekly Bible study. She is also available to speak at Christian events. You may e-mail her at gkkro@embarqmail.com.

Jeannie Lancaster is a freelance writer from Loveland, CO. She is a lover of words, and writes from her heart about life and her experiences raising three children with special needs. She finds joy in simple things, and in quiet moments of reflection and renewal. Contact her via e-mail at bjlancast@msn.com.

Robyn Langdon has a bachelor's degree from Colorado State University and a continuing life degree from Jesus, who teaches her challenging, exciting things every day. She is a daughter of The King, a wife, a mother, a pastor's wife, and a writer — in that order. Visit her blog at www.robynatthecrossroads.blogspot.com.

Debra Larson received degrees from the University of California, Riverside and San Diego State University. She wrote a "Slice of Life" column in her local newspaper and has completed her second young adult novel, which is set in Lake Tahoe where she resides. E-mail her at LarsonDebbie@hotmail.com.

Janeen Lewis is a stay-at-home mom living in central Kentucky with her husband Jesse, son Andrew, and daughter Gracie. When she isn't caring for her children, she can be found writing on her laptop. Lewis has previously been published in three *Chicken Soup for the Soul* anthologies.

Marcia Mansfield spent more than fifteen years as a "modern pioneer," living without electricity or indoor plumbing on remote western property. She and her husband now reside in Denton, MT. Their daughter, **Gayle Mansfield Irwin**, is a writer, author, and speaker with a background in animal welfare. Visit her at www.gaylemirwin.com and www.sagestory.com.

Penny McGinnis earned her bachelor's degree from Franklin University and enjoys working in the local college library as the technical manager. She and her husband enjoy spending time with their grandchildren. Penny likes to read, write, and participate in the women's ministry. To read more of her devotions, visit www.encouragementjourney.blogspot.com.

Cathy McIlvoy's work has appeared in many parenting, Christian, and educational publications and websites. Her first Chicken Soup for the Soul story can be found in *Chicken Soup for the Adopted Soul*. She lives in California with her hubby, four sons, and two ridiculous, yet endearing cats. Drop her a line at cathymcilvoy@gmail.com.

Cecilia McNeal is a native of western Colorado. After returning to her "roots" of farming and ranching, she lived the homestead life in Alaska. Now settled in Kansas, she owns and operates a ranch retreat. Cecilia enjoys her family, skiing, kayaking, acting, museums, and mountain climbing… life! Please e-mail her at cecilia@boxlazya.com.

Michelle Close Mills of Largo, FL, is a wife and mom, and has written for magazines and many short story anthologies, including *Chicken Soup for the Recovering Soul: Daily Inspirations*, *Chicken Soup for the Soul in Menopause*, *The Ultimate Gardener* and *The Ultimate Bird Lover*. Learn more about Michelle at www.authorsden.com/michelleclosemills.

Violet Carr Moore is the author of *In the Right Place* and *Moments of Meditations*, and creator of Carr Twins & Co. (www.carrtwins.com) publishing. She is an inspirational writer and speaker, contributor to a women's ministry website, and vice president of California Writers Club, Tri-Valley Branch. E-mail her at info@carrtwins.com.

Garden enthusiast, avid garden photographer, freelance writer, and inspirational speaker describe **Pat Moyer**. Pat and her husband have their roots in Pottstown, PA, where they have grown two daughters and sprouted two grandsons. Visit Pat's website at www.patmoyer-treasure.net or her blog at www.thegardenwayfarer.blogspot.com.

In college, **Pam Mytroen** vowed that she would never marry a farmer or work with children. She married a Saskatchewan grain farmer the year after she graduated, had four children, and has been directing children's ministries ever since — and she's loving it.

Janice Flood Nichols received her BA from Seton Hill University and her M.Ed. from the University of Pittsburgh. Her stories have appeared in two other *Chicken Soup for the Soul* publications. As a polio survivor, she devotes her time to polio eradication issues. Visit her website at www.twinvoices.com.

Kathryn Nielson received her BA in Communications with a writing emphasis from Moody Bible Institute. She lives in Peoria, IL, with her husband and two children. In her spare time, she loves spending time with her family, reading, drinking coffee, and snuggling with her cat.

Linda O'Connell teaches and writes in St. Louis, MO. Her award-winning poetry, creative non-fiction, and personal essays have been published in twelve *Chicken Soup for the Soul* books, numerous anthologies, magazines, literary journals, and newspapers. Contact Linda at billin7@yahoo.com or www.lindaoconnell.blogspot.com.

Michelle Peters is a social worker and a mother of four. She loves writing and has begun to pursue a career in freelance writing. Michelle has previously published with *Chicken Soup for the Soul* and also wrote weekly for three years for BabyCenter.com. Please e-mail her at peterscnm@hotmail.com.

Michelle Rayburn is a speaker, freelance writer, and musician with a passion for helping people connect the dots between faith, creativity, and everyday life. She has been married for twenty years and loves being a mom of two teenage sons. You may contact Michelle via her website at www.michellerayburn.com.

Shirley Anne Reynolds has published more than fifty magazine and local newspaper articles, led women's bible studies, and is a speaker for women's retreats. Since moving to a rural mountain area, Shirley has come to love riding her ATV over the back roads and hiking the many trails. She is retired and now lives out her passion for writing. E-mail her at heartprints@netzero.com.

Shelley Ring lives near Pikes Peak, CO, with her family and two dogs. She is a "real mom" to her stepson and two biological children. When she isn't playing in the sunshine (and sometimes even when she is), Shelley writes professionally for marketing and publishing industries.

Michelle Rocker is a wife of sixteen years and proud mama of four children. Her journey has taken her down many paths that she never expected, but she believes those exact experiences are forming her writing résumé. You can visit her website at www.michellerocker.com or e-mail her at michelle@michellerocker.com.

Theresa Sanders considers it an honor to be a frequent *Chicken Soup for the Soul* contributor. An award-winning technical writer and consultant, she lives with her husband in suburban St. Louis and is blessed with four beloved grown children. E-mail Theresa at TheresaLSanders@charter.net.

Michelle Sedas is the author of *Welcome the Rain* and *Live Inspired*, and coauthor of *The Power of 10%*. She is the host of the Inspired Living Café and co-founder of Running Moms Rock. Michelle graduated from Texas A&M University, and lives in Texas with her husband and two children.

Marsha Smith worked with a national television broadcasting network for more than twenty years. She received the President's

Award for Excellence twice during that time. She has traveled around the country giving inspirational talks. She continues to spend her time writing and enjoying her grandchildren. Please e-mail her at MSmith336212423@aol.com.

Mary Z. Smith is a regular contributor to the *Chicken Soup for the Soul* series, as well as *Guideposts* and *Angels on Earth* magazines. When she isn't busily penning her praises to God, she can be found in her garden or walking her Rat Terrier Frankie. Mary and husband Barry reside in Richmond, VA, where they enjoy visits from their children and grandchildren.

Ruth L. Snyder is a freelance writer who enjoys writing devotions, articles, and stories. She is a member of the Christian Writers Fellowship and an associate member of The Word Guild. Ruth lives in scenic northeastern Alberta with her husband and five young children. Contact Ruth via e-mail at sun.beam3@yahoo.ca.

Diane Stark is a former teacher turned freelance writer. She is a wife and mother of five. She writes about the important things in life: her family and her faith. She is the author of *Teachers' Devotions to Go.* She can be reached via e-mail at DianeStark19@yahoo.com.

Sharon Struth lives in Bethel, CT, with her husband and two teenage daughters. Her work can also be seen in *Chicken Soup for the Soul: My Resolution*, *Chicken Soup for the Soul: Power Moms*, *Sasee Magazine*, *A Cup of Comfort for New Mothers*, and WritersWeekly.com. Visit her website at www.sharonstruth.com.

Terrie Todd is the mother of three and grandmother to two adorable boys. She and Jon, her husband of thirty-two years, live in Portage la Prairie, Manitoba, Canada, where she is an Administrative Assistant at City Hall. Terrie is also a veteran drama director, actor, and published playwright. Contact her via e-mail at jltodd@mts.net.

Ami Tripp works full-time for the University of California, Davis, and is a wife and busy mother of seven (three are hers and four are his). She is also working on her Master's in Education. In her spare time, she enjoys reading, writing, shopping, and cuddling with her children. Find more of her writings at www.blendingfamilies1.blogspot.com.

Stefanie Wass has been published in *The Los Angeles Times*, *Seattle Times*, *Christian Science Monitor*, *Akron Beacon Journal*, *Akron Life and*

Leisure, *Cleveland Magazine*, *The Writer* magazine, *A Cup of Comfort for Mothers*, *A Cup of Comfort for a Better World*, and seven *Chicken Soup for the Soul* anthologies. Her website is www.stefaniewass.com.

Pam Williams is a freelance writer, pastor's wife, mother, and grandmother of three. Her articles and stories have been published in various cat and Christian magazines, as well as several *Chicken Soup for the Soul* books. She is the author of the book, *Baccalaureate: Guidelines for Inspirational Worship Services to Honor Graduates*.

Marla Woolsey has a Bachelor of Science in Secondary Education and a Master of Science in Engineering Management. Her career history includes mathematics education, systems and manufacturing engineering, and motherhood. Motherhood is by far the most challenging and rewarding. She loves being a mom in south Texas.

Bettie B. Youngs, Ph.D., is a former Teacher of the Year, university professor, and author of thirty-six books published in twenty-eight languages. Her company, Bettie Youngs Books, brings memoirs to film. Contact Bettie via www.BettieYoungsBooks.com.

Melissa Zifzal worked in newspaper and public relations as a writer, designer, and editor before beginning her most important job as a stay-at-home mom. She enjoys reading, writing, and traveling. Melissa and her husband, Dwayne, live in Bloomingdale, OH, with their two sons, Ethan and Caleb, and daughter, Lindsey.

This collection of devotionals was published as a trade paperback in 2010, and has now been published in this beautiful hardcover version. The bios of our contributors were written for the 2010 edition.

Meet Our Authors

Susan M. Heim is a longstanding author and editor, specializing in parenting, multiples, women's and Christian issues. When God unexpectedly blessed Susan and her husband with twin boys, joining the two sons they already had at home, Susan took a leap of faith and left her job as Senior Editor at a publishing company to become a work-at-home mother, which allowed her more time to follow her two greatest passions: parenting and writing.

During the next decade, Susan wrote or collaborated on many books, including eleven *Chicken Soup for the Soul* books; *Boosting Your Baby's Brain Power*; *It's Twins! Parent-to-Parent Advice from Infancy Through Adolescence*; *Oh, Baby! 7 Ways a Baby Will Change Your Life the First Year*; and, *Twice the Love: Stories of Inspiration for Families with Twins, Multiples and Singletons*. Her articles and stories have appeared in many books, websites, and magazines, including *Angels on Earth* and *TWINS Magazine*. Susan also blogged for many years on the topics of parenting and writing.

In 2014, Susan returned to the office as a Library Assistant at her local public library before being promoted to the marketing team where she uses her writing and graphic-design skills to promote literacy and library programs. In her spare time, she continues to edit *Chicken Soup for the Soul* books and recently completed a three-year term as a deacon at her church.

A native of Michigan and graduate of Michigan State University,

Susan loves her adopted home in Florida, where she raised her four sons. Two of her boys have flown the nest, and the other two will follow soon, but Susan plans to continue writing and editing for many years to come while juggling her new obsession with jigsaw puzzles, which she picked up during the pandemic. You can reach Susan through her website at www.susanheim.com.

Karen Talcott is the co-author of four devotional books: *Chicken Soup for the Soul: Devotional Stories for Women*, *Chicken Soup for the Soul: Devotional Stories for Mothers*, *Chicken Soup for the Soul: Devotional Stories for Tough Times*, and *Chicken Soup for the Soul: Devotional Stories for Wives*. Several of her stories have also been included in multiple *Chicken Soup for the Soul* books. When the inspiration strikes, she likes to sit down at her computer with the window open for fresh air and let the story idea take over. She is thankful for her husband, Leland, and three children, Kara, Taylor, and Griffin, for being supportive of her freelance writing.

Karen resides in South Florida and finds her best time to seek God's wisdom is on her morning walks with her beloved Golden Retriever. Story ideas and titles seem to flow as she communes in God's world. In her spare time, she enjoys all moments with her children, their many activities, gardening, walking, and faithfully attending her local church.

Karen wishes to thank Susan Heim for the infamous breakfast years ago when, out of the blue, Susan said, "I feel like God has chosen us to write a devotional." With God's guidance, this book became a vessel for His voice and wisdom spoken through everyday Christian women. Initially, they went from church to church asking women to write a devotional for them. However, God soon took matters into His own hand, and their call for stories spread like wildfire to church women throughout the country. It was exciting to see their idea born out of a cup of coffee turn into an uplifting reminder of God's constant and enduring love for them. Each story selected in this book reminds them that when they put their faith in God, apply His Bible verses to their hearts, and finish with prayer, all things are possible in their lives.

About Lisa Whelchel

Lisa Whelchel was born on May 29 in Littlefield, Texas. At age thirteen, her first professional acting experience was as a Mouseketeer for *The New Mickey Mouse Club*. Ms. Whelchel is perhaps best known for her starring role as Blair Warner on NBC's *The Facts of Life* for nine years.

Her first book, *Creative Correction*, was published in October 2000. The book has sold more than 200,000 copies and received a Gold Medallion Nomination in the Family and Parenting Category.

She is also the author of *The Facts of Life and Other Lessons My Father Taught Me*, *So You're Thinking About Homeschooling*, *The ADVENTure of Christmas*, *The Busy Mom's Guide to Prayer*, *The Busy Mom's Guide to Wisdom*, *The Busy Mom's Guide to Bible Study*, *Speaking Mom-ese*, *Creative Correction — The Bible Study*, *This Is My Story — Bible Study*, and *Taking Care of the 'Me' in Mommy*. Her most recent book is *Friendship for Grown-Ups: What I Missed and Learned Along the Way*.

Ms. Whelchel is married and homeschooled her three children, who have all now left the nest. She feels her current role, as a wife and mother, is her greatest, and most challenging, role yet.

With a goal to refresh and equip other mothers, she is the founder of MomTime Ministries, MomTime Get-A-Ways, and Personal Mom Coaching. For more information, please visit www.LisaWhelchel.com.

Thank You

We appreciate all of our wonderful family members and friends, who continue to inspire and teach us on our life's journey. We have been blessed beyond measure with their constant love and support.

We owe huge thanks to all of our contributors. We know that you pour your hearts and souls into the stories that you share with us, and ultimately with each other. We appreciate your willingness to open up your lives to other Chicken Soup for the Soul readers. We can only publish a small percentage of the stories that are submitted, but we read every single one, and even the ones that do not appear in the book have an influence on us and on the final manuscript. We strongly encourage you to continue submitting to future Chicken Soup for the Soul books.

We would like to thank Amy Newmark, our Publisher, for her generous spirit, creative vision, and expert editing. We're also grateful to D'ette Corona, our Associate Publisher, who seamlessly manages twenty to thirty projects at a time while keeping all of us focused and on schedule. And we'd like to express our gratitude to Barbara LoMonaco, Chicken Soup for the Soul's Webmaster and Editor, and Chicken Soup for the Soul Editor Kristiana Pastir, for her assistance with the final manuscript and proofreading. And yes, there will always be typos anyway, so please feel free to let us know about them at webmaster@chickensoupforthesoul.com, and we will correct them in future printings.

The whole publishing team deserves a hand, including our Vice President of Marketing Maureen Peltier, our Vice President of Production Victor Cataldo, and our graphic designer Daniel Zaccari, who turned our manuscript into this beautiful, inspirational book.

Improving Your Life Every Day

Real people sharing real stories—for twenty-eight years. Now, Chicken Soup for the Soul has gone beyond the bookstore to become a world leader in life improvement. Through books, movies, DVDs, online resources and other partnerships, we bring hope, courage, inspiration and love to hundreds of millions of people around the world. Chicken Soup for the Soul's writers and readers belong to a one-of-a-kind global community, sharing advice, support, guidance, comfort, and knowledge.

Chicken Soup for the Soul stories have been translated into more than forty languages and can be found in more than one hundred countries. Every day, millions of people experience a Chicken Soup for the Soul story in a book, magazine, newspaper or online. As we share our life experiences through these stories, we offer hope, comfort and inspiration to one another. The stories travel from person to person, and from country to country, helping to improve lives everywhere.

Share with Us

We all have had Chicken Soup for the Soul moments in our lives. If you would like to share your story or poem with millions of people around the world, go to chickensoup.com and click on "Submit Your Story." You may be able to help another reader, and become a published author at the same time. Some of our past contributors have launched writing and speaking careers from the publication of their stories in our books!

Our submission volume has been increasing steadily—the quality and quantity of your submissions has been fabulous. We only accept story submissions via our website. They are no longer accepted via mail or fax.

To contact us regarding other matters, please send us an e-mail through webmaster@chickensoupforthesoul.com, or fax or write us at:

Chicken Soup for the Soul
P.O. Box 700
Cos Cob, CT 06807-0700
Fax: 203-861-7194

One more note from your friends at Chicken Soup for the Soul: Occasionally, we receive an unsolicited book manuscript from one of our readers, and we would like to respectfully inform you that we do not accept unsolicited manuscripts and we must discard the ones that appear.

If you found inspiration, peace and happiness in reading this book of devotionals, you will also enjoy *Chicken Soup for the Soul: Devotional Stories for Women*. Following are the first few stories from that book.

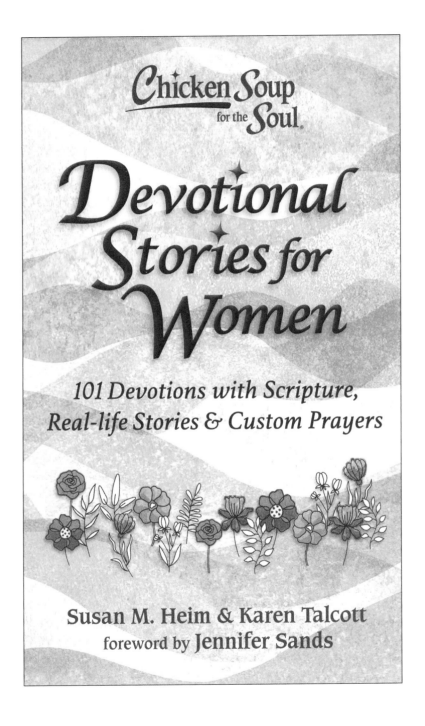

Chicken Soup for the Soul.

Devotional Stories for Women

101 Devotions with Scripture, Real-life Stories & Custom Prayers

Susan M. Heim & Karen Talcott
foreword by Jennifer Sands

1

A Cool Breeze and a Change of Heart

I will praise you, O LORD,
with all my heart; before the "gods"
I will sing your praise.
~Psalm 138:1

Living in Florida, the summer heat wears on you after awhile. The mornings start in the nineties with high humidity, and the days end in the eighties with high humidity. I often feel that our seasons are reversed from the rest of the country. About May, we tightly close up our houses and put on the air conditioner. Then we live inside for most of the summer heat. Around the end of October, the beginnings of a few cool fronts make it down to our state.

So, our expectations were high when we learned that the weatherman had forecast the first blast of cool air coming our way one night. How excited my husband and I were to open the windows in anticipation of the fresh air. That night, I awoke to the fresh breeze flowing around me. It felt so lovely to be snuggled up and yet have that hint of cold around me.

The next morning, my whole family felt alive. We were playful at breakfast while the dogs bounced around at our feet. We dug out our "cool weather clothes" for the first time in months. It was funny to laugh at how our favorite clothes had shrunk. Had my son's legs really grown that long over the summer?

With the kids off to school, I headed out for my morning walk with the dogs. The cool weather made me walk faster, and I felt so invigorated. I listened to the birds calling in the trees, watched the busy squirrels, and admired the beautiful flowers. These had all been the same sights the day before, but today my eyes were fresh. My heart filled with gratitude for the beloved garden that God created.

I think it is important to savor those moments when you really feel alive. What makes you wake up and start the day in anticipation? It could be as simple as a day of cool weather. Regardless, it is God's way of catching our attention and honoring this truly magnificent world He created.

— Karen Talcott —

My Prayer

God, what a truly wonderful world you have created! You had a master plan behind it all, and I am so fortunate to be a witness to your creation each and every day.
Amen.

2

From Fruit of the Loom to a Car

*God sets the lonely in families... You gave
abundant showers, O God; you refreshed your
weary inheritance. Your people settled in it,
and from your bounty, O God,
you provided for the poor.*
~Psalm 68:6a, 9-10

When my husband and I decided to start a family, we budgeted, planned, and scheduled. Moving from a dual-income family to a single-income family was a major adjustment, but we felt it was worth the sacrifice for me to be home. We were not sure how we could make it work, but we were ready to try and felt in control.

Eight months after our daughter was born, while we were still adjusting to the changes that had occurred, God brought two precious boys, ages five and six, into our lives. The boys came with nothing, but we felt called by God to have them in our family. We adopted them, not knowing how we could provide for a family of five on one income. We had an old car that needed replacing, quite a few bills, and no extra cash, but a lot of love.

We were in awe as God provided, meeting needs as they became apparent—and often before they were even apparent. God used so many people to bless us. Our Sunday school class and my husband's employer held showers to welcome the boys to our family. Our one attempt at buying new things for them resulted in the purchases being rung up at no cost, including their Fruit of the Loom underwear! Regularly, we would find anonymously sent cards of encouragement with cash gifts.

A church family even gave us a car, and over the years as the used cars have died, we have been given two more from completely different families. One year, each student in my husband's fifth-grade class brought a gift for someone in our family and filled the space under our Christmas tree.

Our leap of faith has been a blessing as we watch God provide and direct our lives. We have since added another beautiful daughter to our family. We still attempt to plan, and things frequently do not go as expected, but God has provided abundantly and continues to provide. Clearly, He is in complete control.

— Robin Smith —

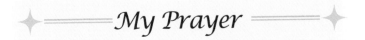

My Prayer

*Dear God, please help me to trust your direction
and provision. I am so thankful
that you are in control.
Amen.*

3

A Blessing in Disguise

So do not fear, for I am with you; do not be dismayed, for I am your God. I will strengthen you and help you; I will uphold you with my righteous right hand.
~Isaiah 41:10

We were just leaving the movie theater when, out of the blue, I turned to my roommate and said, "I'm not going to have a job tomorrow."

She freaked out. "Why?! Don't say that!" she said.

I told her, "God just popped 'fear not, nor be dismayed, be strong and of good courage' in my head, and told me I wouldn't have a job after tomorrow."

She looked at me as if I'd lost my mind and said, "You're weird." Then we went home.

Strangely, there was nothing wrong at work. I had just been gone for a week traveling for my job, and I hadn't even been back to the office yet. But everything had been fine when I was last there. However, I'd known for a while it was time to move on. I just didn't have the courage to leave. I even talked to God about it in prayer and asked Him to either give me the courage or make it happen.

The next day, I went into the office just like normal. I wrote on a card the verse God had given me outside the movie theater and put it up on my office wall. Everything was fine until 5:00 P.M. My boss called a meeting. He said that times were hard, and he would be laying off some people and decreasing the salary of others.

We went into our offices, and he went around to let each person know what their fate would be. When he came into my office, I smiled and said, "I know! God told me yesterday, and I told my roommate! See, here's the verse!"

He was shocked and said, "But I didn't even think about it until today!"

The next three months were an exhilarating time of change for me. The entire direction of my life changed in ways I couldn't even hope for while I was still at my previous job. That loss turned into one of the biggest blessings in my life.

— Lorie Bibbee —

My Prayer

God, you are so good! Thank you for preparing and providing. You really do make a way when there seems to be no way, and bring hope when all hope seems gone. Lord, thank you for giving me courage, and I pray for anyone who is facing major change now. Please let them see your hand clearly.
Amen.

Changing lives one story at a time ®®
www.chickensoup.com